Trusting Through Suffering

Trusting Through Suffering

Leon J. Wood

with Shirley R. Hull

This book has been prepared primarily for group study in connection with the Adult Teacher's Guide available for $1.50 from Regular Baptist Press. However, it is an excellent and informative book to use for individual instruction.

Published by
REGULAR BAPTIST PRESS

1300 North Meacham Road
Post Office Box 95500
Schaumburg, Illinois 60195

About the Authors

This course of study was written by the late Leon J. Wood. It was originally published in January 1965 and has been revised for republication at this time.

Before his death in 1977, Dr. Wood was professor of Old Testament Studies at Grand Rapids Baptist College and Seminary, Grand Rapids, Michigan. In addition to his teaching ministry, Dr. Wood instructed multitudes of people through his writing ministry. He wrote several adult Sunday School courses for Regular Baptist Press, as well as the book *Elijah: Prophet of God*. Dr. Wood's works were also published by other publishers. He was working on two books at the time of his death, and these have recently been released by Baker Book House: *The Prophets of Israel* (co-published by Regular Baptist Press) and *Israel's United Monarchy*.

This course revision was prepared by Shirley R. Hull, curriculum writer and conference speaker for Regular Baptist Press.

Contents

Foreword / 7

Family Devotional Times / 9

1. Job, the Man / 13
2. Satan, the Adversary / 22
3. Job Tried / 31
4. Job's Friends / 39
5. Job's Despair / 49
6. Eliphaz: Sowing and Reaping / 58
7. Bildad: Greatness of God / 67
8. Zophar: Man's Dependence on God / 75
9. Job Perplexed / 84
10. Reflection and Trust / 93
11. Elihu Speaks / 103
12. God Himself Speaks / 112
13. Job Rewarded / 121

© **1979** by Regular Baptist Press. Vol. 28, No. 2. Printed in U.S.A. Merle R. Hull, Executive Editor.

Foreword

TRUSTING THROUGH SUFFERING is the story of Job, a man approved of God. It is the story of a man who, because of intense suffering, asked "Why?" But he learned to trust his God even though the question went unanswered. It is the story of a man of faith who looked forward to the coming of his Redeemer; who, in spite of inaccurate counsel, kept his eyes fixed on the God of Heaven.

What believer has not gone through times of mental, physical or spiritual anguish? What saint has not at some time been tempted to cry out, "Why, Lord?" The Book of Job will be a source of help and encouragement as you see anew the greatness of the God you worship, His power throughout the universe He made, His sufficiency in every experience of life. Read the book for information. Then read it again to discover the riches God's Spirit placed there for your blessing and instruction.

Learn the weekly memory verse and read the daily Bible readings. Give special attention to the family devotional ideas. Learn, if you do not already know them, the blessings and benefits that can come from Bible reading and prayer in your home.

Let this study change your "Why?" to "Thy will be done."

Family Devotional Times Made Interesting and Practical

"WE'VE STARTED FAMILY devotions at our house. In fact, we've started family devotions a million times!" exclaimed the disturbed father. "We have them for a few days. Then something happens and we stop. What shall we do?"

There is only one solution. Keep on starting! Set a goal for yourself and your family for this quarter. Start and maintain a daily time of Bible reading and prayer. It won't be easy. Satan knows what a benefit it could be to your family. He won't let it be easy. But you can do it—with God's help. Here are some ideas to help you in your goal.

1. Plan your time with the ages of your children in mind. Use Scripture they can understand. For young children, use Bible storybooks as well as the Bible. Keep passages brief. Explain words.

2. Use variety: visuals, playacting, pictures, chalkboard, flash cards, slides, films.

3. Let different members of the family plan and lead devotions.

4. Keep prayer requests current and practical, expecting results.

5. Keep the atmosphere relaxed. If one person is out of sorts, don't demand that he take part. Keep discipline separate from the devotional time. Don't use it as an opportunity to preach to the children, but rather as a time when the Word speaks to the entire family.

6. Be honest in all discussions. Admit sins and mistakes. Admit questions; then search out the an-

swers and solutions from the Bible.

7. Use your children's Sunday School lessons as guides for devotional material.

8. Be flexible to meet the daily requirements of schedules, activities and temperaments.

9. Let children tell how the Scripture applies to their lives.

10. Distribute crayons and paper so each family member may draw a picture of the lesson taught.

11. Learn the books of the Bible. Have Bible spelldowns, Bible word searches, Bible sword drills.

12. Learn Bible geography and relate it to current events. Read the newspaper with the Bible in mind.

13. Make assignments for family members to work out before the next devotional period.

14. Memorize Scripture verses (the weekly memory verse).

15. Give a thought for the day—a poem, quotation or easily remembered phrase.

16. Put a chalkboard in a prominent place and write on it the thought for the day. Different family members could submit new thoughts.

17. Provide a family bulletin board on which to place missionary letters and pictures, prayer requests, cartoons, poems, handwork, special honor papers, prayer answers, letters to be shared, family notes and other interesting items.

18. Teach missions through devotional times by using missionary letters, pictures and stories. Have missionaries in your home.

19. Provide good Christian literature to be read by the entire family and discussed together.

20. Put up a calendar. Each day after Bible reading and prayer, allow one member to mark through that day. Each week, compare the number of days

marked off with the previous week's record. See how many days you can read without missing, trying to better each previous record.

21. For variety, have a songfest on some theme; a hike in the woods, noting God's goodness; a visit, including prayer and Bible reading, with a shut-in; an original story or poem written by a family member; a testimony of God at work.

22. Challenge each family member to have private devotional times. Share these blessings with the family.

General Suggestions: The head of the house should establish and maintain Bible reading and prayer. A mother with an unsaved husband can still have Bible reading and prayer with her children, including him if he desires, or planning the devotional time in a way that will not bring dissension or resentment. Perhaps it will be necessary to have Bible reading and prayer with each child.

Don't be frightened by the words *family altar, family devotions* and the like. These phrases simply speak of a regular time when the family reads God's Word together and prays that God will help each one to obey the Word read.

You need the food, the fellowship and even the fun that can be a part of gathering as a family around God's Book. But you must make an effort. As Job of old, continually seek the face of God for the spiritual good of your family.

CHAPTER 1

Job, the Man

BIBLE PORTION TO READ: Job 1:1-5

SUPPOSE YOU NEED to apply for a job. Whom will you ask to recommend you? An enemy? Of course not! An enemy might lie about you. A friend? That would be better. He would surely show you in a good light. Maybe he would even overlook some of your flaws. Yes, maybe a friend would give you a good recommendation.

But what if God were to write a recommendation for you? He is wholly honest, wholly good. He cannot sin—or tolerate sin. He is just and righteous. He knows all about you, even to the hairs that fall from your head. What would God say about you?

Christian, aren't you thankful that God looks at you through the righteousness of His beloved Son? Aren't you glad that you have been washed white in the blood of Calvary's Lamb?

Sinner, you don't have that righteousness. God sees you in your sin: hopeless, defiled and away from Him. But He loves you and offers you pardon through His Son. Will you receive Him and be saved?

> There is welcome for the sinner,
> And more graces for the good;
> There is mercy with the Savior;
> There is healing in His blood.
> *F. W. Faber*

I. Job's Origins

No one knows for certain when or where Job lived, nor does it matter. The book itself does not provide this information, so an inquisitive student of the Word must search for clues that might reveal it. If you are such a student, think through the answers to these clues:

Where, according to Job 1:1 and 3, did Job live? What people lived near enough to raid his herds? What culture is represented by the way Job's wealth was measured? By the fact he sat with his friends for seven days? Why do you think that, in all the deliberations about suffering, no mention was made of the great suffering Israel experienced in Egypt? Why weren't the laws and ceremonies given to Moses at Sinai mentioned? What does Job's age at death suggest about when he lived?

II. Job's Character (Job 1:1, 8; 2:3)

Imagine the scene in Heaven which is depicted in perhaps the oldest book of the Bible. The Lord in all His glory was receiving the sons of God. Satan came also with them. The Lord began to recommend one of His followers, a man from Uz named Job. And this was His evaluation!

Job was perfect. The Hebrew word means "whole" or "complete." The dictionary defines the word as expert, proficient, entirely without fault or defect. This was Job in God's sight. He was not

> **A Verse To Memorize**
>
> "There was a man in the land of Uz, whose name was Job; and that man was perfect and upright, and one that feared God, and eschewed evil" (Job 1:1).

sinless. Only the Lord Jesus Christ, God Himself incarnate in the flesh, can claim perfection. But, according to the Lord, Job lived an unusually righteous life, one devoted to God.

Job was upright. This word is often used to describe a straight road or an even path. Job exhibited a strict regard for all that was morally right. He was honest, just, conscientious, scrupulous and honorable. He lived in accordance with the will of God.

Job feared God. He did not try to hide from God. Rather, he held God in a sense of reverential respect. Fear in the sense of dread views the one feared as an enemy. Fear in the sense of respect considers him a friend. Job was a friend of God.

Job eschewed evil. He shunned it, turned aside from it. He avoided sin as a habit of life. Read Romans 12:9 for the New Testament principle.

Read again God's evaluation of this man, Job. It would be difficult to find four better ways to characterize a God-pleasing life. Believer, do you measure up? Are you willing to reverence God and to turn aside from evil? When you do, your life will become upright and your way perfect.

SOME SCRIPTURES THAT WILL HELP
A necessary beginning—Ephesians 2:4-10
A dedicated heart—Ephesians 3:14-21

A pleasing walk—Ephesians 4:24—5:10
A sure defense—Ephesians 6:10-20

III. Satan's Attack (Job 1:6-12; 2:1-7)

Since the time of original sin, Satan has been intolerant of one who tries to live for God. Satan's goal has been—and will be until his final defeat—to bring all creation under his power. When he saw the upright, perfect Job, Satan challenged God to allow him to prove that Job would fall if the right circumstances and trials were given to him.

Notice, Satan did not look for a weak, vacillating person to attack. He chose a godly, exemplary man who was approved by God. It would be greater glory for Satan for a strong man to fall.

His ways have not changed. Satan is interested in the godly believer, the thriving church, the productive Bible school and college, the fruitful mission field. He will do all in his power to cause them to fall to his wiles.

When things are going well and you can see the hand of God at work, beware. Christians sometimes become complacent in times of victory. The temptation is to pray less when days are bright. If anything, you should pray more, remembering that each victory is from the Lord.

Is there encouragement in this for the believer who is going through difficulties? Yes! It could be that Satan is attacking you because you are doing something right; you are accomplishing good things for God. Satan would not be interested in you if you were useless.

IV. Job's Family (1:2-5; 2:9; 19:17)

Job had a wife. She is mentioned twice in the book, showing what sort of person she was. Both

> **Daily Bible Readings**
>
> Sunday — Riches and Pride — Luke 12:16-34
>
> Monday — Riches and Death — Luke 16:19-31
>
> Tuesday — Poor Use of Money — Luke 15:11-24
>
> Wednesday — Right Treasure — Matthew 6:19-34
>
> Thursday — Father Instructs a Son — Proverbs 4:1-27
>
> Friday — Mother and Son — 1 Samuel 1:10-28
>
> Saturday — A Good Wife — Proverbs 31:10-31

references depict her in a poor light. In Job 2:9 she asked Job to "curse God, and die." This was exactly what Satan wanted Job to do.

Read Job 19:17. Evidently she turned from Job because of his foul breath. He begged her not to reject him, if for no other reason than the memory of their children. It is clear that she was no help to her husband, but a hindrance. G. Campbell Morgan has suggested that perhaps she reacted as she did, not because she was a poor wife, but because she loved him and did not want to see him suffer such agony. Death would be welcome, and she, in her love, was willing to let him die in order to free him from his suffering. In either case, Job's marriage partner could have been a great comfort, but apparently she was not.

Choosing one's life partner is important. For believers, marriage is forever. Young people, your most important decision, after salvation from sin, is the choice of a marriage partner. It would be better never to marry at all than to choose a mate who will lead you away from God and into a life of distress and fruitlessness.

Married people, it is your responsibility to make every effort to help one another; to lend encouragement and comfort in time of need; and to seek together to help your family experience the blessings and joys of a truly Christian home.

In addition to his wife, Job had seven sons and three daughters, a happy family who met together for feasting and fellowship. They enjoyed being with one another. Too often children look everywhere except to the family for companionship. In some homes, family members scarcely seem to be able to talk together even about trivial matters—much less about the vital issues that concern each one. It should be the goal of every Christian family to make the home a place for love and comradeship between children, as well as mutual respect and communication with parents.

God established the family unit and is pleased with family togetherness. Think of some ways you can improve this condition in your home. List these ideas here.

_____
_____
_____
_____
_____
_____

Job served as priest for his family. Read Job 1:5. What did Job do each time his children gathered for a celebration? He wanted them to be present when the sacrifice was made to show their interest and their approval of his offering. Also, he may have wanted his sons to help prepare the animals for the sacrifice. Job set the example. It should have prompted his family to refrain from sin and to serve God. It was a practice for his children to follow when they had families of their own.

What a fine thing if all fathers were this interested in the spiritual welfare of their children! Too many do not even know where their children are; much less do they gather them for family worship. Fathers, Job set the example for sacrifice and service.

Job sacrificed for his family continually. He did not let circumstances hinder or time defer. Most believers are good beginners at Bible reading and prayer. Many, however, do not carry through what they begin. Family devotional times are begun and then stopped because other things, usually important things, interfere. Satan knows your family will benefit from spiritual activities, so he makes them difficult. Continual family altars will count for eternity. "Thus did Job continually."

V. Job's Possessions (Job 1:3)

Job was very rich. His wealth, not counted in money and lands but in animals, made him the greatest of all the men of the East. He was the rich man of his day, and, with all his wealth, he loved and served the true God. Not many were like this outside the line of Abraham, but Job was one. He stood among his neighbors as the greatest in wealth and the greatest in spiritual values.

Read Mark 10:23. When one is rich, he is tempted to trust in his wealth and not in God. Wealth tends to make one independent and self-sufficient. Riches become the center of one's thinking; getting more wealth becomes the object of life. Spiritual matters do not concern him. Consequently, few rich people are won for Christ. And of those who are, few become strong, spiritual leaders. Thank God for the exceptions—people who receive the riches of this earth and use them in humbleness of spirit to expand and enlarge the work of Christ through their local churches and throughout the world. Jesus did not say that no rich persons enter the kingdom of God. Job is a shining example of one to whom God could entrust great wealth.

God can use those who have talent to make and handle money. Such men normally have good business acumen, and God's work needs to be operated in sound, businesslike ways. Every aspect of God's work needs spiritual men of wealth to work alongside spiritual men of less affluence. Think of the need for adequate finances for Christian service. How many young people wait to go to mission fields? They are prepared and eager, but they lack money. How many schools are understaffed? How many small, struggling churches need their own buildings? How many social agencies must curtail their ministries—all for the lack of money? Rich men who love God as Job did are needed today.

But God was not interested in Job's wealth. Look again at the characteristics He presented to Satan. Did He mention Job's wealth? Job's great riches did not serve to make him acceptable in God's sight. He was accepted and commended because of spiritual qualities. He was perfect, upright, feared God and eschewed evil. God does not measure His children in terms of their bank accounts or possessions. He measures in life and conduct and devotedness to Him in obedience and service. In a short span of time, Job lost all his wealth and earthly treasure. In just a short span, you could lose all that you have. But when Job's wealth was gone, all that mattered to God remained.

Somehow, we think of the man with money and position as more important in the church. Not God! On this count, all God's children are on equal ground. God looks on the heart.

When He looks at you, what does He see?

What Is Your Answer?

1. Will you sincerely try to begin family Bible reading and prayer this week?

2. What proof can you find in the New Testament that God will not let Satan tempt you more than you are able to bear?

3. What counsel does this lesson present to young people? To parents? To the rich? To the poor?

CHAPTER 2

Satan, the Adversary

BIBLE PORTION TO READ: Job 1:6-12; 2:1-7

"HE'S GOT THE whole world in His hands"; and "He's got you and me, brother, in His hand!" All power belongs to Him. All things were made by Him. All things are maintained by Him Who is the Lord of lords, the omnipotent, omniscient, omnipresent God. Nothing can befall His child without first receiving His divine permission. Remember these truths as you look at Satan's attack on Job.

Remember, too, that it was God Who called attention to His outstandingly righteous servant, Job. God put him on display as one who was perfect and upright, who feared God and avoided evil. God was in control in all the events of Job's life. He had lessons for Job, his family, his friends and for you and me that could only be taught by allowing Job to experience them.

Surely, Satan was there. Satan was working. But in all he did, God was in control, putting up His hedge and ready to give His help and supply. Today Satan is showing his power and doing his work in ways that have not been displayed before. Churches have been established in his name; people around the world worship him. Some Christians are so afraid of him that they think more of his working than of the power of their great God.

Satan plays a prominent role in the story of Job, and we can learn much about his person and tactics. It is important to know these things in order to be forearmed against his attacks.

I. The Person of Satan

See the heavenly scene. The sons of God came to present themselves to the Lord. Among these sons, or angels, was Satan whose name means "the accuser." Read Zechariah 3:1 and 2; Isaiah 14:12-17. Satan was a fallen angel. He was cast out of Heaven because he tried to be like God. He was a brilliant angel prior to his fall, and since then he has been the leader of the angels who fell with him.

This fallen angelic being has great power—far more than man. With all his power, however, he is not infinite as is God. He cannot be in more than one place at a time (omnipresent); so he must work through other fallen angels named demons. Nor is Satan all-powerful (omnipotent) or all-knowing (omniscient). These attributes belong only to our great and wonderful God. Satan is simply an imitator, but such a clever one as to make it necessary for every believer to be in constant and close fellowship with his Heavenly Father.

II. The Domain of Satan

Job 1:7 finds Satan "going to and fro in the earth, and . . . walking up and down in it." John 12:31 identifies Satan as "the prince of this world," and

> **A Verse To Memorize**
>
> "Be sober, be vigilant; because your adversary the devil, as a roaring lion, walketh about, seeking whom he may devour" (1 Pet. 5:8).

Ephesians 2:2 names him "the prince of the power of the air." Satan is free to move about in this world. He has access to your home, your business, your church, your social gatherings. He has access to your dining room table when you try to have family devotional times. He has access to your shop or office when you try to witness. He is, in fact, able to be everywhere you go. He observed Job, and he observes you today. Satan is very real. Be keenly aware of him.

When you remember that Satan was once cast out of Heaven, it is difficult to realize that he yet has access there. But read Job 1:6 and 2:1. These verses mean Satan entered Heaven at this time. He was cast out of Heaven as a resident. He no longer could live or work there. He could not fellowship with God. But he did return to communicate with God.

III. The Work of Satan

Memorize 1 Peter 5:8. This graphically describes the work of Satan. Picture a ravaging lion, stalking about looking for prey. This is Satan. He has actively opposed God's will and work since his fall from Heaven. He is against anything God is for. If you are *for* God—working *for* Him, living *for* Him, trying to win others *for* Him—then Satan is against you too.

Satan was against Job because Job was for God.

Satan accused Job, which is one of his chief activities. It is a fine commentary on Job that Satan was unable to point out any specific sin in his life. It should cause us to hang our heads in shame at the amount of sin with which he could charge us before God. Regarding Job, all he could say was that Job served God because of the abundant way God provided for him.

It was Satan's goal to make Job sin. To achieve this, Satan was willing to hurt Job in any way. Satan is no friend of man, though often man thinks he is. In man's own desire to sin, he finds greater affinity for Satan than for God. Satan desires to have it just this way. However, Satan is man's enemy, wishing him no good, but willing to bring him to the lowest degradation in order to accomplish his ends. How many derelicts and suicide victims thought Satan was their friend when they first started on their downward slide!

Satan first attacked Job's wealth. He knew the rich normally value their wealth above all else. This did not work with Job because he had fixed his interest in God rather than in his possessions. Satan is clever and attacks his victims according to their weaknesses, but his attack on Job's wealth failed. Then Satan took Job's family, but this was no more successful. Still not deterred, Satan attacked Job's body, bringing terrible suffering. People will do almost anything to alleviate bodily pain. Satan knew this well and exploited the fact in Job.

We need not wonder, then, why it is difficult to have victory over our weaknesses. Satan works on them, relentlessly tempting us to walk in his way, the broad way of destruction and sin. Think of your life. What are your weaknesses? Concentrate on them. Ask God to give you strength to defeat the

> ### Daily Bible Readings
> Sunday — Resisting Satan — 1 Peter 5:1-11
> Monday — Eve's Temptation — Genesis 3:1-7
> Tuesday — Cain's Failure — Genesis 4:1-15
> Wednesday — Abraham's Test — Genesis 22:1-14
> Thursday — Jesus and Satan — Matthew 12:22-30
> Friday — Defeat of Believers — Acts 5:1-11
> Saturday — Jesus Defeats Satan — Matthew 4:1-11

onslaughts of Satan, the accuser of your soul.

IV. The Power of Satan

Satan has power to influence people. Read Job 1:15 and 17 to see how he influenced the Sabeans and the Chaldeans to do his work against Job. These two groups of people carried out Satan's bidding. They did what he wanted. Satan has power over the human mind. He cannot force it to make wrong decisions, but he can influence it by persuasion to do so. He persuaded Eve to eat the forbidden fruit (Gen. 3:1-6); he persuaded Judas to betray Christ (John 13:2); he persuaded Ananias and Sapphira to lie to the Holy Spirit (Acts 5:3). Here he persuaded two raiding bands to attack Job's herds at this particular place and time.

Satan also has control over the elements in nature. He brought fire to burn Job's sheep and wind to kill his children. The Bible often represents nature as under God's control, but in this case, it seems that Satan commanded and the elements obeyed.

This seems to be a contradiction. How can both God and Satan control? And if Satan can control, how can we safely trust in our God? The answer is that God does indeed exercise the final control, but He gives permission at times to Satan to do so. Read 2 Thessalonians 2:9 to find a time in the last days when Satan will perform seemingly mighty acts. But God is in control. Satan is limited by that control, and his ultimate end is damnation.

Satan brought attack on Job's body, so he has power to send sickness; again, of course, only as permitted by God. We may believe from this example in Scripture that God does allow him to tempt by sending sickness. Do you become easily discouraged because of ill health? You may be a likely subject for Satan's attacks to your body.

For all of Satan's power as seen in the life of Job, defeat is possible. God gives the formula in James 4:7. Memorize this important instruction. What are the two action verbs to you if you are a believer in Christ? Submit and resist! Give yourself to God in total submission. Let Him control you. This is your action toward God.

Then, do something toward Satan: resist him! God's weapon has two sides: your responsibility to submit and your necessity to resist. God will do it all, but He will do it through you. He will give you strength, courage, wisdom and all you need to resist Satan in every area of your life—when you submit in total obedience to Him. How does Satan tempt you? Admit it to God. Submit it to God and He will give you the victory as you resist through His power. "Now thanks be unto God, which always causeth us to triumph in Christ . . ." (2 Cor. 2:14).

V. The Limitations of Satan

Satan complained to God that a protective hedge sealed Job from any temptation that would cause him to curse God. Satan said this hedge needed to be removed before he could bring his attack. See the precious truth for the believer. God protects His children from the unhindered attacks of Satan. The word used for "hedge" means a fence to keep out marauders. Job and his possessions were safe from Satan so long as the hedge remained.

God knew Satan's strategy, but He acceded to the request nevertheless. He only removed the hedge in part. The first time He took enough of it away to allow Satan to attack Job's possessions and family; the second time, to attack his body with disease. Even then, God did not let Satan take Job's life (2:6). The hedge was removed at God's direction. God was in control.

When Baptist Mid-Missions missionary Irene Ferrell died at the hands of terrorists in Africa, her parents surely could have cried out, "Where were You, God? Why weren't You in control?" But He was there, working out His perfect will.

When national pastors on one of our mission stations were buried alive at the hands of wicked men, their wives could have turned in dismay to beg, "Why don't You save them, Lord?" But God was there, giving comfort and courage. He was in control. From those persecutions He has raised up believers who are stronger than they could ever have been without the suffering and trials. He has proved His all-sufficient grace in the hard places of sorrow.

Yes, God is in control. Though Satan bears the title, "prince of this world," he does not have absolute control. He is under the control of God. God created the universe and superintends it. He is ever working out His plan in it. Satan can do nothing to thwart that plan. Be joyful. When you look around and see sin abounding and great dictators defying God, you may cry out, "Where are You, God?" But God is working out His purpose in spite of Satan's greatest efforts against Him.

With God in control, Satan can do only what God permits. Satan himself acknowledged that God had put the hedge about Job. Not only is that fact true, but it is also a fact that God holds Satan on a leash. Satan has power within the compass of the leash, but only that far; and God can check him any time He wishes. Read 1 Corinthians 10:13. God is in control of Satan and will allow him to tempt you only as you can bear it. No more. What a glorious truth for the believer. Times of temptation can be times of despair—or times of victory. God wants them to be times of victory through Him.

VI. God's School of Faith

Since God truly knows you, He knows how weak you are. Why, then, does He allow temptation at all? Why did He permit Satan to tempt Job? Why does He permit trials in our lives that bring these times of temptation?

The answer is plain. God sees these trials and temptations as a school of faith by which His children may develop in their Christian experience. Satan intended evil for Job; he wanted Job to sin. God intended the temptations for Job's good. He wanted Job to grow yet stronger in his life of faith.

Christians grow in faith by making right decisions. The harder it is to make such decisions, the stronger our faith becomes. The decisions then become steps of progress. Our spiritual lives mature. This thought was in Paul's mind when he wrote,

"But we glory in tribulations also: knowing that tribulation worketh patience; And patience, experience; and experience, hope" (Rom. 5:3, 4).

Our walk with God becomes more devoted and our dependence on Him increases when we are tested and show ourselves true. As we grow, we can be entrusted with yet more difficult tests. Remember this truth when you see some of God's choice servants suffering. Don't make the mistake of Job's friends and charge them with great sin. God may be leading them to a deeper relationship with Himself.

Remember this truth, too, when trials and testings come to you. Examine your life and conduct to make certain you are God's kind of person. Then, trust God to control all the elements of your life as you take steps of progress in His school of faith, always seeking to be a good student for Him.

What Is Your Answer?

1. Why does God allow testing and trial to come into the believer's life?

2. Why does Satan not attack all believers in the same way?

3. How may a person resist Satan?

CHAPTER 3

Job Tried

BIBLE PORTION TO READ: Job 1:13—2:10

AN OLD MAN, bent arthritically over his cane, hobbled down the steps of the funeral home and out to the sidewalk. His face mirrored the sorrow of his heart. He had just buried his wife of forty-three years, and the loneliness he felt burdened him with such remorse that he could scarcely move himself along. As he neared the corner, he saw a small boy, no more than seven or eight, leaning against the lightpost, crying in great despair. "Why do you cry so?" asked the old man.

"I've lost my silver dollar," cried the little boy. "I can't find it anywhere, and it is the very best thing I own. What will I do without my shining silver dollar?"

The old man reached out in sympathy to pat the young head. As he walked slowly away, he thought, "Son, you cannot know what loss truly is!"

Everyone experiences loss, sorrow and trial; some more than others. But all, no matter their age, know the trials of daily living.

Anyone who reads Job's story must admit he suffered more than most people in a short span of time. This suffering and the lessons it teaches us are the reasons Job's story is in the Bible. In spite of his suffering, Job remained faithful to God. His life provides an outstanding example to encourage you in days of distress and perplexity. Give careful attention, child of God, to the nature of Job's testing and the manner of his victory.

I. Satan's First Attack (Job 1:13-22)

You remember, of course, that Job was an exceedingly rich man, richest of all the men of the East. His wealth was counted in animals, and these filled the fields and roamed the desert stretches for miles around. His life's work was represented in those animals. Think of the planning and labor that had gone into accumulating and caring for them!

But on the day Satan went before the Lord and decided to tempt Job to curse God, Job's herds and flocks were in danger. Read Job 1:13-22. Job's sons and daughters were at the eldest son's home, having a celebration. Scripture does not say where Job was, but it is certain he was not at the party.

While they were celebrating, a messenger came to Job. Surely in much agitation, he exclaimed that while the oxen were plowing and the asses were feeding nearby, the Sabeans (probably a predatory tribe out of the Arabian Desert) fell upon them and took them away, killing all the servants with swords. "And I only am escaped alone to tell you," reported the messenger.

Even before the first messenger had stopped talking, a second messenger arrived. "The fire of God is fallen from heaven, and hath burned up the sheep, and the servants, and consumed them." And again,

> **A Verse To Memorize**
> "In all this Job sinned not, nor charged God foolishly" (Job 1:22).

as had the other messenger, this one added, "And I only am escaped alone to tell you."

Seven thousand sheep and all the shepherds— gone. Dead. Burned to death by fire, probably lightning sent to destroy.

Even as he told of the terrible fire, another messenger ran to Job and said, "The Chaldeans sent out three bands, and fell upon the camels, and have carried them away. Yes, and they killed the servants with swords; and I only am escaped alone to tell you."

Three thousand camels taken by roving bands of Chaldeans. In later years, the Chaldeans became strong in number in Babylonia; and even the great Nebuchadnezzar, king of Babylonia, was a descendant. Apparently on this day they had split into three groups to make a surprise attack on Job's herds. Or possibly the camels were grazing in three herds.

Within a matter of minutes wealthy Job was destitute. The news came so fast he had no time to adjust his thinking to one loss before another was upon him. Had Job centered his life in these possessions, he would have reeled and fallen before such an onslaught of bad news.

What would your reaction have been? Honestly, now, could you have taken such a sudden tragedy? Some people consider their wealth their chief interest in life. Their first thought on any given day is the condition of the stock market, international trade and the like. Some Christians even fit into this group. Every drop in the economy causes them distress.

Jesus warned against laying up treasure on earth. Read carefully Matthew 6:19-21. If money tempts you, memorize the verses. Treasure laid up in Heaven does not fade. It cannot be lost; therefore it does not bring disappointment. Treasure laid up on earth may fade; it can be taken away. It will lose value and often causes sorrow. Money is not sinful. We must have it to live in this world. A great deal of money is not wrong. It can, indeed, be a blessing when it is dedicated to God. How about your money, Christian? If it were taken away, could you still praise God?

Job not only lost all his wealth—he lost his lovely, happy family. Satan continued his trial through the dearest treasure Job possessed. A fourth messenger came to Job and said, "Your children were at your eldest son's house. A great wind came from the wilderness, smote the four corners of the house, and it fell; and they are dead. I only am escaped to tell you."

The wind must have been a twisting tornado. Such a storm generates terrific speed in its circling motion. It can easily tear a house to pieces and cause it to fall. Anyone who has experienced such a calamity well knows its terror. Satan struck the home when the young people were gathered for their party and killed them outright. (We believe the term *young men* meant "young people," including both brothers and sisters.)

Job's loss was great. No longer would he offer sacrifices for his children. They were dead. This

> **Daily Bible Readings**
>
> Sunday — Suffering — Exodus 1:7-16; 2:23-25
> Monday — Furnace of Fire — Daniel 3:8-30
> Tuesday — A Picture of Christ — Psalm 22
> Wednesday — Gethsemane — Matthew 26:36-46
> Thursday — The Shepherd Psalm — Psalm 23
> Friday — Faith As Gold — 1 Peter 1:1-9
> Saturday — Under His Wings — Psalm 91

trial was worse than his loss of wealth. What was his reaction in 1:20-22?

Mourning the loss of loved ones is not wrong. It is natural to miss them and not a shame to show it. Read 1 Thessalonians 4:13. Paul did not mean we do not feel the loss. But we may, along with our sense of loss, rejoice because our loved ones are with the Lord. The loss is ours, not theirs.

Job mourned, yet he worshiped God. He showed a triumphant heart when, in spite of his bereavement, he did not criticize or show bitterness. He submitted to the will of God and worshiped Him. What an example for you and me! Read again his prayer from a broken heart:

> Naked came I out of my mother's womb,
> And naked shall I return thither:
> > The LORD gave, and
> > The LORD hath taken away;
> Blessed be the name of the LORD.
> > *Job 1:21*

Satan's confident assertion to God had proven altogether false. Job's reaction to the terrible temptation is given in one concise statement: "In all this Job sinned not, nor charged God foolishly." Job did not sin. Nor did he charge God with unfairness or injustice, which, indeed, is foolishness.

II. Satan's Second Attack (Job 2:1-10)

It likely was not long before Satan made his second request of God. He would not have wanted the intensity of the first suffering to lessen before he brought the second. This time Satan asked permission to strike Job's body. God gave permission, but He put up a hedge so Satan could not take Job's life.

Have you ever had a boil? If so, you know that even one small infection of this sort can bring intense discomfort. Satan smote Job's body with "sore boils from the sole of his foot unto his crown" (v. 7). Job's condition required that he go outside the city to sit on the ash heap where, in his misery, he scraped his sores with broken pottery.

In this degraded, agonizing condition the once mighty Job heard his wife say, "Do you still retain your integrity? Curse God, and die."

"Haven't you had enough? How much more can you be expected to take? What good is it doing you to try to hold out? You might as well give up and die. I can't stand to see you suffer more." Since she was a wife, she probably raised her voice and wrung her hands and cried great, sobbing tears. And why not? Had Job suffered all the loss? It was her wealth too.

But look at Job. With running sores racking his body and a wife reminding him of his loss, still he was God's man—perfect, upright, fearing God and avoiding evil. What an example he continued to present!

> Why could Job stand? His eyes were on God. How can YOU stand? Keep your eyes on God.
>
> 1. Know you are His—Romans 3:23; John 3:16; Romans 5:7, 8; Acts 16:31; John 1:12.
> 2. Know His Word—1 Peter 2:2; 3:15; 2 Timothy 3:16, 17; Psalm 119:9-11.
> 3. Know how to pray—2 Thessalonians 5:17; James 1:5; 5:16.
> 4. Know how to submit—1 Corinthians 6:19, 20; 2 Corinthians 5:17.
> 5. Know how to resist—1 Peter 5:8-10.
>
> These verses, when studied and applied, will help you to stand for God. The Bible explains God's way for you. Study it every day, for in it you will know God. ". . . The people that do know their God shall be strong, and do exploits" (Dan. 11:32).

Job spoke out of his distress, "You're talking like one of the foolish women would talk. What do you think; shall we receive good at the hand of God, and not receive evil?" In all his talking, Job did not sin with his lips. Job was willing to take loss and pain along with the blessings God had given, knowing that God does all things well.

W. E. Sangster tells the story of an ungodly man, full of self-pity at his lot in life, who read a bright, confident article in a paper. He tossed it aside in disgust, complaining that whoever wrote the article had never suffered as he had. Then the story of the author came out. Early in his career he contracted an incurable disease and was confined to a wheelchair. Six years later his devoted wife, on whom he so completely depended, died of cancer. He was left with two young children to raise in spite of his crippled body. Yet he was able to write with joy and confidence because, as a friend wrote, "He *really* has religion. I've heard him talk of Christ in a way that left me in no doubt that he knows Him personally, quite friends in fact."

Unpleasant experiences of life often provide great spiritual benefits for the believer who will keep his eyes fixed on the Lord. When you are tested and tried, take time to think, to take inventory of your life. Recognize afresh your degree of dependence upon Him. Remember the extent of His great grace.

Job did not sin; he did not do what Satan wanted. He proved that his faith in God was genuine, not fixed in the blessings he had received.

What Is Your Answer?

1. What does Job's reaction to his losses show about his attitude toward them?

2. What would your attitude have been?

3. What lessons have Job and his wife taught you?

CHAPTER 4

Job's Friends

BIBLE PORTION TO READ: Job 2:11-13; 32:1-6; 42:7-9

> I'VE FOUND A FRIEND, O such a Friend!
> He loved me ere I knew Him;
> He drew me with the cords of love,
> And thus He bound me to Him.
> And round my heart still closely twine
> Those ties which naught can sever,
> For I am His and He is mine,
> Forever and forever.
>
> I've found a Friend, O such a Friend!
> So kind and true and tender,
> So wise a Counsellor and Guide,
> So mighty a Defender!
> From Him who loves me now so well,
> What power my soul can sever?
> Shall life or death or earth or hell?
> No—I am His forever.
>
> *J. G. Small*

Do you know this Friend? Have you found peace with God by believing that this Friend died to take the punishment for your sins? "Greater love hath no man than this, that a man lay down his life for his friends" (John 15:13). Christ loved you and laid down His life for you. What a Friend is He!

God has made us social creatures. We need fellowship. God planned fellowship for us with family and friends.

Some of the most miserable people in this world are those who have no friends. At one time or another, probably everyone feels friendless and alone. The distress of loneliness causes problems that are well-known to counselors, for it drives many to the brink of despair. Often the friendlessness is not real. Some around us want to be friends, but we will not have them. Sometimes no one truly cares. How wonderful, then, to call out in prayer and reach out in faith to the One Who longs to be a friend that sticks closer than a brother.

Look now at Job. He needed a friend if anyone did. He had once been the mightiest man of the East, owning thousands upon thousands of herds and flocks and all the wealth they provided; having a strong, healthy family of seven sons, three daughters and a loving wife. There he sits—on an ash heap, his robe dirty and torn, and his body covered from head to foot with oozing, throbbing sores. He was destitute of all except his wife and his suffering.

Into this hopeless scene came three friends who had heard of Job's plight. Like Job, they were rich and noble men. They had made an appointment to go to their friend in his time of need, to mourn with him and to comfort him. Time was to show that the friends actually caused more hurt than help. In future chapters, each friend and his speeches to Job will be examined separately; but now look at them

> **A Verse To Memorize**
> "Now when Job's three friends heard of all this evil that was come upon him, they came every one from his own place . . . for they had made an appointment together to come to mourn with him and to comfort him" (Job 2:11).

together and see how they failed. Learn from them for times when God gives you the opportunity to be a friend and comforter to one in need.

I. Identity of Job's Friends (Job 2:11; 32:1-6)

Remember their names because you will meet them often as you walk through Job's book. Three came together, and later a fourth joined them. Of the three, Eliphaz the Temanite was easily the most important. His name has been defined as "God is strength" or "God is fine gold," suggesting the greatness and preeminence of God. He always spoke with courtesy. As you read his speeches, you will respect him as a sensitive gentleman.

Bildad, the second speaker, was an arguer who wanted to fight. Even his name means "son of contention." You've known Christians like him—always right, always ready to prove it at any cost and to fight if you disagree.

Then there was Zophar. His name is said to mean "a sparrow." Zipporah, Moses' wife, bore the feminine form of this word. Zophar's speeches are almost rude in their bluntness. He did not use tact or finesse in speaking, but he did not speak with much enthusiasm either.

Elihu arrived after the three, but evidently early enough in the discussions to hear most of what was said. He was younger than the others; so he waited until the others finished before presenting his long, interesting speech.

II. Their Interest (Job 2:11-13)

The three friends had heard of Job's terrible troubles, but it is doubtful they ever imagined they would find him as they did. When they came near enough to see their noble friend, they wept. They tore their expensive robes and sprinkled dust on their heads—signs of mourning. Then, showing extreme humility—considering their wealth and renown—they sat down in the ashes with Job and silently offered their comfort for seven long days and nights.

Who can tell what Job must have felt at the nearness of these who had come? Though Job does not give us the answer, we know that burdens become lighter when the burdened one knows that others care enough to sympathize. In the hurry of the present day, it is easy to neglect this Christian ministry. But God notices when we express our sympathy to those in need, and He is pleased.

> Christian, how long has it been since you:
> Called on a sick friend?
> Went to a funeral home to give comfort?
> Took a token of friendship to one in need?
> Offered sympathy to a troubled saint?

Eliphaz and his friends made an effort to be with Job. They were not just passing by. They had to plan the journey and, by appointment with one another, go to Job's side, each from his own place

> **Daily Bible Readings**
> Sunday — Psalm of Comfort — Psalm 103
> Monday — Comfort of Jesus — John 14:1-31
> Tuesday — Joy — Philippians 1:8-30
> Wednesday — In Christ — 2 Corinthians 5:1-10
> Thursday — Hope — 1 Thessalonians 4:13—5:11
> Friday — Judge Not! — Matthew 7:1-12
> Saturday — God's Glory — John 9:1-41

(2:11). They inconvenienced themselves to be with their friend. They humbled themselves to stay with their friend.

How many Christians do you know who are ready to put themselves out to help another? A couple in a midwestern town have through the years planned ways to help their pastor above and beyond their tithe. They paint and wallpaper the parsonage when it is needed, keeping their good works to themselves. They take food to church members in need. They stop by to help when a fellow member has a broken washer or leaking plumbing. They do not act with fanfare or a desire for attention, but because they feel this is one way they can serve Christ. You see, Christ saved them after they were married and had a family. They feel their youth was wasted, and they want to do all they can with the years that remain.

In a small church in the east, a single lady made it her responsibility to help young people who had given their lives to Christ for His service. She could not do much above her giving to the church, but she could provide some material blessings to lighten the load—things like small radios, tickets to concerts, well-balanced meals and smiling encouragement.

You've known some people like these. Perhaps you are one. These people will shine in a special way when God's rewards are read. They know the meaning of His injunction, "Thou shalt love thy neighbour as thyself" (Mark 12:31). This involves more than money or material goods. It requires forethought, time and effort.

Read Job 2:11 and 12. Do you think the sorrow expressed by the three friends was genuine or hypocritical? Job had been their respected friend, honored by all. Now he was in this pitiable condition. Both surprise and sympathy would have contributed to the intense emotional display of the three. Too, this was the customary mode of mourning in that time and place as, indeed, it still is today.

Having displayed this outward evidence of mourning, "they sat down with him upon the ground seven days and seven nights" (2:13). This amazes us today. How could anyone sit for this length of time? And why seven? See Genesis 50:10 and 1 Samuel 31:13.

They not only sat, they sat *silently*. This is probably more amazing. Out of respect for Job and the extent of his suffering, they remained silent, refraining from talking about his grief. This does not mean that they did not talk at all, anymore than that they sat without moving all the time. But they did not speak to him about his affliction, or of other things except as current need required. They sympathized with him in quietness.

Many words are not necessary to express sympathy. Often we err in speaking too much, in telling our own experiences. The suffering one cares little about our troubles. He has enough of his own without trying to deal with ours. Our troubles seem like nothing to the one who is in the center of his own overwhelming problem. Silent fellowship is more of a healing balm than words without wisdom.

III. Their Character

Eliphaz, Bildad, Zophar and even Elihu were intelligent leaders in their communities. No doubt they had wealth comparable to Job's, though his had been the greatest. It is apparent they had servants to do their work because they could take time to be with Job.

Each of the men showed himself a true product of his country. The philosophic nature of the Arabian nomad has long been known, and these men reflected it as they gave their answers to Job. They had keen minds and demonstrated a love for careful distinctions in thought. As you read their speeches, you may gain the impression they were all saying the same thing. Yet, each one approached Job's problem in a different way. As this study proceeds, make certain you read each of the speeches. You will enjoy knowing the unique manner of each man.

These men had reputations of moral uprightness. Otherwise, they would hardly have accused Job as they did. Sometimes those most guilty are the first to accuse others, but these men would not have done so. Job could have used this as a point of retaliation if they had been known sinners. Probably they were moral and proud of their reputations. It gave them authority to condemn Job as they did.

It is easy to become proud of one's reputation. A person should value his reputation, but not be proud of it. How did Christ feel about this (Matt. 23:27)? Be careful to avoid this "righteousness" of the Pharisees!

In spite of their faults, these men were true believers in God. They spoke highly of Him. They erred concerning Job, but not God. Bildad, for instance, asked, "How then can man be justified with God? or how can he be clean that is born of a woman?" (25:4). And Zophar questioned, "Canst thou by searching find out God? canst thou find out the Almighty unto perfection? It is as high as heaven; what canst thou do? deeper than hell; what canst thou know?" (11:7, 8). An unbeliever would not have spoken in this fashion.

These men were theologically correct but practically wrong. They could describe God's greatness, but they could not understand a fellow man's sorrows. They could not put their head knowledge into action with heart demonstration. This is a common fault. Many people know about religious matters, but they fall far short in practicing them. Knowing all the Bible teaches about purity is important; being pure is more so. Knowing all the Bible teaches about love is important; demonstrating that love is God's purpose for the believer. The list could go on. God desires Christians who believe the Bible's message and then go out to live it. Is knowing easier than doing? Is doing more blessed? Try it. You will find your life enriched as you practice what you know for God's glory.

IV. Their Procedure

What do you think Eliphaz, Bildad and Zophar were thinking during those seven days and nights as they sat beside sick, suffering Job on the ash heap? You can be sure they were meditating with all the resources of their wisdom, trying to unravel the reason for Job's troubles. Job, too, was thinking. All were asking in their minds the universal question, Why?

Were these men, then, so different from you and me? We would have thought and conjectured—probably without so much silence. And we would have come to the same *why*. Job knew his heart; he knew he was right before God and truly trying to do God's bidding. The friends by now had probably decided that Job was not what they had thought. Future speeches bear this out.

So, after seven days and nights of silence and meditation, Eliphaz, Bildad and Zophar arose from the ash heap to end their time of mourning with their suffering friend. Did Job think they were leaving him alone? Did he dread sitting without their comfort? Had his meditation finally brought him to the place of crying out? Whatever the reason, as the friends ended their time of mourning with him, Job opened his mouth and began to curse.

Job spoke first in each of the three cycles of speaking. The order each time was: Job, Eliphaz; Job, Bildad; Job, Zophar; with one exception—Zophar did not take his last turn in the last cycle. Job spoke at length, then Elihu. Job spoke a total of twenty chapters; Eliphaz, four; Bildad, three; Zophar, two; and Elihu, six. How they needed the words of Paul, "Let your speech be alway with grace, seasoned with salt . . ." (Col. 4:6).

V. Their Contention

Though each of the friends approached Job's problem from his own viewpoint, their basic contention was identical: Job had sinned grievously and was being punished. They believed the only reason for such suffering was punishment from God. Job, then, must have sinned. They based their thinking upon a scriptural principle: what a man sows, he reaps. However, these men erred. They did not consider any other explanation and were quick to condemn him.

Never condemn another simply because he suffers. It may be punishment from God, but it may also be for other reasons. Too, if it is punishment from God, it is for the person suffering to recognize. Read Matthew 7:1 for good advice.

Because these friends condemned Job, they were reprimanded by God (42:7-9). Thus, Job was vindicated by the highest Judge. God knows each of His own perfectly. He judges justly. There will be many surprises when we stand before the Savior. The humble will be exalted and the self-righteous abased. God knows the heart and rewards accordingly. How important to be approved by the Lord in the last day! This will be approval that counts.

What Is Your Answer?

1. How would you classify Job's friends as to their spirituality?

2. How would you commend his friends?

3. What are criticisms you can find of them?

4. Think of several ways you can show true friendship during the coming week.

CHAPTER 5

Job's Despair

BIBLE PORTION TO READ: Job 3:1-26

EIGHT YEARS HAD PASSED since John, the local blacksmith, had turned from a life of terrible sin to new life in Christ. One day as he pounded a piece of molten steel, one of the town's businessmen, who had watched John change from the local troublemaker to a regular church attender, stopped to watch John work. "John, it seems to me you have had nothing but trouble since you started going to that church over there. I thought when you started going to church and thinking about that God you talk about all the time, you'd have things easy. What kind of a God gives you so many trials and accidents?"

John was quiet as he held up the piece of steel he had been pounding. Then he spoke quietly, "You see this piece of steel? Before I can use it, I have to heat it red hot in the fire. Then I push it into cold water where it sputters and cools. If I find it can take a temper, I heat it up red hot again. Then I hammer and bend and shape it, and after a while this piece of steel will be tempered just right to be a spring for your wagon."

John hesitated, then continued, "The way I see it, God saved me for more reason than just to have a good time and go to Heaven. I'll get that for sure. But just like this steel, God needs to temper me so I can work for Him. So He lets me have tests and trials and troubles. He'll supply the strength and help so I can learn to be strong for Him."

The study of Job shows this perfect and upright man being tempered as surely as that steel. For seven long days and nights Job had sat on the ash heap outside the city, a place reserved for the unclean and diseased. With him were the friends who had come to give silent comfort and to mourn with him.

Now the time of mourning was over. The friends could go their way. But Job, crying out in despair, ended the silence and cursed the day he was born.

Those words of despair pose a problem for the student of this man, Job. How can his utter despair be reconciled with the plain statements that Job sinned not found in Job 1:22 and 2:10?

I. Job's Words of Despair (Job 3:1-26)

Probably everyone has said at one time or another, "I wish I'd never been born." No one ever said it with such passion as Job did. To pronounce a curse is always a serious matter. In the last analysis, of course, only God can curse. Man is inclined to express deep feelings by cursing (see Jer. 20:14); but Paul warned us to "bless, and curse not" (Rom 12:14).

Job wished evil upon the day he was born. No singing, "Happy birthday, dear Job." He did not share the opinion that his birthday was something to

> **A Verse To Memorize**
>
> "After this opened Job his mouth, and cursed his day" (Job 3:1)

celebrate. He pronounced a curse upon it, wishing it were:

> Death instead of life.
> Darkness instead of light.
> Blotted by God from history.

Was it all right for Job to wish that his day of birth had never occurred? Job was wrong. He sinned! God is in charge of history. He has an overall plan for it, and nothing can frustrate His divine plan. Many things happen which we cannot understand, but somehow every experience, each event, all fit into the plan He has worked out for His great glory.

It is not for us, then, to wish away any day, whether of our birth or any other. We should say with the psalmist: "This is the day which the LORD hath made; we will rejoice and be glad in it" (Ps. 118:24). At times we will feel as Job did. Life's pressures will press upon us, driving us to the point of despair; but let us not give way to sin.

But, you say, Job did sin. How can I, who certainly cannot be described as perfect, do better than Job? Read carefully 2 Corinthians 12:9 and Ephesians 4:7.

Job not only cursed the day of his birth, but the night also. He wanted to be sure that, whatever the time of his birth, a curse was pronounced upon it. He wanted the night to be so dark it could not be joined to any following day. These verses are the only place in the Old Testament where *blackness* is used. It means the blackness that comes, for example, from a total eclipse of the sun (as witnessed in the state of Washington during the last total eclipse of this century in February 1979). The word is used five times in Job. In the Hebrew language, four different words were used to express the intensity of Job's feelings.

Job felt he had a reason to be bitter. The day he was born made possible these present days of suffering. No man, especially one of Job's stature, normally talks as Job was talking. Before the trials allowed by God and given by Satan, he had realized how much he had for which to be thankful. He was wealthy, wise, honored by all, had a fine family, and enjoyed the approval of God. After having all that, he wished now he had never been born.

Job left the pronouncements on his birthday to reflect on the advantages that would have been his if he had died on the day he was born instead of living to come to such agony. Most of us fear death and do all in our power to stay its day. But on this day, Job thought death sounded attractive. Instead of agony on the ash heap, he would be at rest, quiet and sleeping in the company of "kings and counsellors of the earth" and "princes that had gold, who filled their houses with silver" (3:14, 15). Death is an equalizer. Rich and poor will be on equal footing in death.

Job's friends had not said a word at this point. However, Job must have sensed in them some critical attitudes. He felt that even in their silence they were troubling him.

As you read Job's curse on his existence, you find

> **Daily Bible Readings**
> Sunday — Victory — Romans 6:1-23
> Monday — God in Control — Romans 8:28-39
> Tuesday — Hope — 1 Corinthians 15:20-34
> Wednesday — Victory — 1 Corinthians 15:35-58
> Thursday — Sins — Numbers 15:24-31
> Friday — David's Sins — Psalm 19:7-14
> Saturday — Prayer for Forgiveness — Psalm 51

him going from one figure of speech to another, sometimes using several in a sentence. If he were dead, he would have rest. He would be like the kings in death. He would get relief as prisoners get relief from unjust oppression, and servants from their masters. Job cried for relief from his prison of suffering and his master of misery.

Was Job right in his evaluation of death? Is it right for us to long for death? The answer is no. The Christian is to look forward to life with Christ throughout all eternity and to anticipate it with joy. Perhaps you have heard the old question, "Are you homesick for Heaven, or just sick of living?" Believers should never look forward to death merely as a cessation from misery. God knows about our suffering. He will give grace to bear it. It is not for us to take matters into our own hands, as if to help God. This would logically lead to suicide. Rather, we must submit to God's will and trust Him to work out what He sees is best.

What, then, is the purpose in suffering? Why

must the righteous suffer? Job asked, "Wherefore is light given to him that is in misery, and life unto the bitter in soul?" (3:20). As you read Job 3:20-23, you will hear Job say that suffering people long for death, digging for it like hidden treasure and rejoicing when they find it. You will hear him ask why life is given to a man when he doesn't know why things are as they are, or what his purpose in life should be. Job implied that the reason these things are true is because God has "hedged" him in from knowing.

The answer to the basic question of why a man must suffer cannot be found in Job's anguished cries. It must be seen as God's training school of faith. Through suffering, God trains and equips His children for greater spiritual maturity. Times of trial become times of spiritual development. When we experience hardship, we cast ourselves more on God's grace. We learn to submit to His will. We are reminded of our own frailty and dependence. We see Him as the supreme Ruler over all. When our faith is tested, it is challenged to grow. We must believe in God's goodness while experiencing trouble. We must learn to say His way is best, even though at present it is unpleasant. We grow more through trial than through prosperity. We may be sure that Job grew through his. He was a fine child of God before this suffering experience; but without question, he was yet better afterward.

Remember, the book was written in poetic form. Many of the phrases are poetic in nature. For example, when Job said he sighed before he ate (3:24), he may have meant he sighed continually. Or it may mean he experienced anguish from swollen lips and caked sores. At any rate, because of it, Job's "roarings" of pain were "poured out like the waters."

Job closed his speech by remembering how suddenly his trials had come upon him. As he heard of one, he feared for the next; and sure enough, it came. He was sure these losses had not come from negligence on his part. He had not thought himself so safe that he had rested instead of being vigilant. He had not invited the losses. He had taken adequate precautions, and still they had come. Evidently this fact preyed on his mind and made the losses yet harder to understand.

Job had been right in taking precautions. When Jesus said, "Take therefore no thought for the morrow" (Matt. 6:34), He did not mean we are not to plan ahead. He meant only we are not to worry and fret. We are to plan and use our good judgment in taking proper precautions; but when we have done all we should, we must leave the matter with God. This is the way of trust. To worry implies a lack of confidence in God.

II. Job's Despair in Relation to His Righteousness

Job 1:22 and 2:10 both say Job did not sin in connection with his trial. However, we have seen Job saying things that were wrong and sinful. How can these two facts be harmonized? Did Job sin in connection with this trial or not? If he did, what do the two statements mean which say he did not? A few observations help us understand.

Job did sin in his despair. One cannot curse his day, wishing it had not occurred, without challenging God's righteous supervision of history; and this is sin. We cannot be God's critics. The answer is, then, Job did sin.

However, Job did not sin in the way Satan said he

would; he did not curse God. Quite the contrary, Job always maintained an exceedingly high opinion of God, saying, for instance, God "is wise in heart, and mighty in strength" (9:4); or again, "If I justify myself, mine own mouth shall condemn me" (9:20). Job's sin was less than Satan desired. Job did complain of his sad state but without any intended criticism of God. And even this came under extreme duress of suffering.

This implies that God sees a difference in the seriousness of sin—a truth we need to recognize. Jesus said it would be more tolerable for Tyre and Sidon at the judgment than for Chorazin and Bethsaida where He had displayed mighty works (Matt. 11:20-24). In other words, when a person or city has had the advantage of greater light, their sin is more serious. Again, the Old Testament draws a difference between sins of ignorance and sins done presumptuously (Num. 15:24-31). Sacrifice could be made for sins of ignorance, not for sins of presumption.

Job's sin was clearly a sin of ignorance. That is, he did not plan to sin, neither was he fully cognizant he was criticizing God. In his suffering, the complaint came forth without premeditation. Accordingly, it was much less serious than a clear renouncement of God predicted by Satan.

However, any sin is serious enough; and Job did sin. Seven days had passed since the words of 1:22 and 2:10. The indication that Job did not sin is in reference to his first response to his terrible losses. Satan had hoped to overwhelm Job by the rapidity of his losses and his extreme suffering, and so make him sin. Job took the shock and gave glory to God. He had so girded his thoughts during his life that he was able to withstand Satan's blows. His spiritual reflexes were trained through years of godly living.

Job maintained himself at first, but he did not hold back the sin during longer suffering. If this were true of a man of Job's stature, we must take warning. Pressure builds in times of unending suffering. A sort of limit of endurance is reached.

God takes circumstances into account when His child sins. God spoke highly of Job both before and after this experience (42:7, 8), in spite of his sin. God does not excuse His sinning child because of circumstances, but He does understand human frailties and the strength of temptations. In His grace and goodness He provided His own Son to be our sympathetic High Priest. Though He is God, He "was in all points tempted like as we are, yet without sin" (Heb. 4:15; see also 2:18). He gave His promise to be "faithful and just to forgive us our sins" (1 John 1:9) when we confess.

How about your spiritual reflexes? Do you have the personal assurance that God is in control and does all things well?

What Is Your Answer?

1. Why should you thank God for trials?
2. Why is sin worse to a person with more "light"?
3. Is premeditated sin worse than a sin of ignorance? Why?

CHAPTER 6

Eliphaz: Sowing and Reaping

BIBLE PORTION TO READ: Job 4; 5; 15; 22

ONE DAY MRS. MARY, a Christian farm woman who lives in Peru, South America, came to missionary Jennie Adams. "There is no work to do in the fields," she said. "It didn't rain, so we cannot plant. I think the Lord would like me to do some planting for Him. No one has planted among the people back in the hills behind the mountains."

So Mrs. Mary, carrying a good supply of tracts given to her by Jennie, went to the people back in the hills behind the mountains where no roads are. Several months later she returned, carrying a box with records of what she had done during her planting for the Lord. Twelve men, eight women and five children had studied 205 Bible lessons. Seven men, six women and three children had written in their lessons that Mrs. Mary had led them to the Lord. As they studied, their lives were changing. Others who were not fortunate enough to know how to read and write had also heard the gospel message. Later a child asked Mrs. Mary to "hand her over" to the Lord. She recognized she was a sinner. Mrs. Mary explained that Christ had already died to pay for her badness.

Mrs. Mary had gone out to sow for the Lord, planting His life-giving Word in the hills behind the mountains. What a harvest she reaped!

Have you ever planted for the Lord? Have you had the blessed experience of sowing His Word and reaping precious souls for His glory? "He that goeth forth and weepeth, bearing precious seed, shall doubtless come again with rejoicing, bringing his sheaves with him" (Ps. 126:6).

One of Job's three friends had a theory about sowing and reaping. He, too, believed that whatever a man sowed, he reaped. Conversely, if a man reaped something bad, he must have sown something bad. Look at Job. Job was reaping suffering and loss. He must have sown sin. Eliphaz was in error when he insisted that this principle of sowing and reaping explained Job's trouble.

The coming chapters deal with Job's friends. Look now at Eliphaz. Review the facts you learned about him in chapter 4. Eliphaz presented three speeches. You will find his first speech in Job 4 and 5, his second in Job 15 and his third in Job 22. Read these chapters before you continue.

I. Eliphaz Criticized Job (Job 4:2-5; 15:2-6, 11-13)

In the opening of his first speech, Eliphaz told Job that, though he had often instructed others to stand in the face of trials, yet he was not able to so stand. To a degree, Eliphaz was right in this; but two things should be said in Job's defense. First, his suffering certainly was far more severe than any others Eliphaz could have had in mind. Second, a man can usually encourage someone else better

> **A Verse To Memorize**
> "Even as I have seen, they that plow iniquity, and sow wickedness, reap the same" (Job 4:8).

than he can encourage himself. Persons who have been greatly used to encourage others often sorely need help from others in their own times of distress. Think of someone you know (perhaps yourself) of whom this could be true. Are you ready and willing to say and do the thing that will help that one over the hard places of trials? Seek out opportunities to show yourself a true friend to those in need.

When Eliphaz spoke the second time, he accused Job of speaking empty words. According to his criticizing friend, Job's talk was unprofitable and his own mouth condemned him. These were hard words to be spoken against a man of Job's intelligence. Others listened to him with great respect. Obviously this charge against him showed that Eliphaz did not understand Job's condition or the reason for it.

Are you ever tempted to criticize or advise someone who is going through deep waters? Choose your words carefully. Consider what the person has endured and what experiences have been his. Try to understand the person and his needs. Pious platitudes spoken without understanding may only add to his distress. Try to place yourself in the position of the one you wish to help. Saying nothing is better than saying the wrong thing.

Eliphaz even accused Job of being against God—an untrue statement. How did Eliphaz arrive at this falsehood? He and his friends had tried to console Job. Job had turned his back on their advice and had not accepted it as the reason for his suffering. So Eliphaz concluded that since Job had not accepted what the friends had told him, he had turned against God. True, the friends had spoken about God and principles of God, but they were not speaking the words of God. Job knew they were wrong; he would not accept their worthy principles as accurate reasons for his suffering condition.

Many today assume what they say is the dictum of God Himself. The one who dares to go against their advice is going against God. Remember, however, the only inspired words God has given us are those in His Word. He has given us His Spirit to indwell us and to teach us how that Word applies to us in every experience in life. He teaches us in our hearts.

> Are you reading God's wonderful Word every day? Let it speak to you so you will know His way for your daily walk.

Inspiration does not give infallibility to the statements of Eliphaz and his friends, or even those of Job. It simply insures the accuracy of the record of those statements.

II. Sowing and Reaping (Job 4:6-9)

Most of Eliphaz's speaking centered in the principle that whatever a man sows, he reaps. This, of course, is scriptural (Gal. 6:7). God does not overlook sin. The Flood came in Noah's day as God's punishment for the wickedness of that day. In eternity, great and terrible punishment will fall upon all who do not accept the Lord Jesus Christ as

> **Daily Bible Readings**
> Sunday — Sowing and Reaping — Galatians 6:1-10
> Monday — Vengeance — Romans 12:17-21
> Tuesday — The Flood — Genesis 6:5—7:24
> Wednesday — Nebuchadnezzar — Daniel 4:28-37
> Thursday — Unchangeable God — Malachi 3:1-6
> Friday — Righteousness — Deuteronomy 28:1-14
> Saturday — Wickedness — Deuteronomy 28:15-68

Savior. Today this principle is being worked out in the lives of men and women, boys and girls who suffer as the consequence of their sin. So Eliphaz presented a scriptural viewpoint to Job.

However, there are exceptions to this principle. All who sin do suffer; but not all who suffer do so because of sin. It was not Job's sin, but his outstanding righteousness, which brought about his suffering. Eliphaz did not know this, and he allowed for no exception to his rule of sowing and reaping. It was not his work to judge Job. This still is true. Never pass judgment on others as to the cause of their trials and troubles. Pass judgment on yourself, but not on others.

III. All Reap Suffering; None Are Just (Job 4:17-21; 15:14-16)

Eliphaz asserted that all men, without exception, are sinful. God finds "folly" in angels (4:18); and so

He finds it in men who dwell only in "houses of clay" (4:19). Also, God cannot put trust "in his saints. . . . How much more abominable and filthy is man, which drinketh iniquity like water?" (15:15, 16). Heaven saw impurity when Satan aspired to be like God. Eliphaz's point was if impurity was found in those, how could Job think himself pure?

What is the truth Eliphaz presented? All men are sinners. No person is pure. Christ alone lived a spotless life. Read Isaiah 64:6. Because of the sinlessness of the Savior, He could die for sinful man; thus any man may be righteous in God's sight. "Who his own self bare our sins in his own body on the tree, that we, being dead to sins, should live unto righteousness: by whose stripes ye were healed" (1 Pet. 2:24).

IV. God Will Not Change (Job 5:1-5; 22:2-5)

Job's case was hopeless, according to Eliphaz. He might as well forget about praying. God would not help him. His laws do not change simply because a man cries out. Could God be persuaded to change because a mere man asked for help?

What do you think? Was Eliphaz right? Does it mean anything to God that His children live righteously? The answer to this is clear: the righteous lives of God's children mean much to Him. Otherwise, the Bible would not stress godly living.

Can God be changed by the heart cry of the believer? This answer is not quite so simple. In the last analysis, God never changes. He is unchangeable (Mal. 3:6; Heb. 13:8). Yet God clearly promises to answer prayer, and He repeats this promise many times. (See John 14:13.) Our prayers and His eternal purpose work together to accomplish God's perfect will.

V. Remedy: Submit to God (Job 5:6-11; 22:21-25)

Read Job 5:6-11 and 22:21-25. In the first passage, Eliphaz speaks of the certainty of trouble for man; but, he concludes, if man submits to God, the trouble will be lessened.

In the second passage (from his third speech), Eliphaz says that peace comes by acquaintance with God. Thus, trouble will be lessened and obvious blessing will come to the one who becomes acquainted with God.

What was Eliphaz saying to his friend? If Job would submit to God, he would be relieved of his suffering. He would have his material wealth restored.

Submission to God is good advice. Eliphaz did not speak a false principle. Every Christian should desire to be completely submitted to God. How God's work needs men and women who are willing to say with the poet, "All that I am or hope to be, I surrender it all, O Lord, to Thee."

This is the way to peace and blessing, and God Himself will determine whether the blessing will be material or spiritual. Job was seemingly an exception to this rule, but only temporarily so. After his trial great blessing returned to his life, both spiritually and materially. God was not working on the same time schedule as Eliphaz and his friends. But God was caring for His faithful servant. He knew Job's heart and planned for his reward. God's timetable was right for His glory and Job's good. His timing is still best for His faithful servants today.

VI. The Results (Job 5:12-27; 15:20-25; 22:26-30)

Look at all the blessings Eliphaz, in his first

speech, assured Job would be the portion of all who were righteous before God (5:12-27):

Salvation from the sword
Binding up of wounds
Salvation from famine, war, destruction
Peace
Children and long life

In his third speech, Eliphaz continued to present the blessings to expect (22:26-30):

Knowing God hears prayer
Seeing well-laid plans work out
Being able to help others

In his second speech, Eliphaz dwelt on the aspects of punishment God would send to the wicked who "stretcheth out his hand against God" (15:20-25):

Having pain
Being attacked by the destroyer
Seeking food in darkness

VII. Job's Situation (Job 22:6-18)

Eliphaz used most of his third speech to enumerate Job's sins (22:6-11). He assured Job that God looked down from Heaven. He knew all about Job's wickedness (22:12-14). Dark clouds could not conceal from God the truth that Job had sinned anymore than dark clouds before the great Flood could conceal the people of that day (22:15-17).

So the first of Job's comforters revealed what he considered to be the cause of Job's great distress. What is the summation of his conclusions? Job had defrauded people to gain his immense wealth. God, Who sees all from Heaven, had seen Job's wickedness. For punishment God had taken all that Job possessed. Job was being judged for his sin because, reasoned Eliphaz, whatever a man sows, he must reap.

Knowing the complete story of Job and his suffering, it would be easy to say that Eliphaz was cruel and bad in his passionate denunciation of Job. But Eliphaz was not bad. He had come as a friend. He was, though, terribly mistaken. His advice was inaccurate. His conclusions were pious, personal opinions. He thought of himself as an oracle of God, apparently expecting Job to cry out in repentance.

Surely we can learn from Eliphaz—so wise in his own conceit; so ignorant of God's purposes and ways. God's Word says, "Judge not, that ye be not judged" (Matt. 7:1); and again, "So then every one of us shall give account of himself to God" (Rom. 14:12).

What Is Your Answer?

1. What Bible characters illustrate the truth of reaping what is sown?
2. Does prayer move God to act on our behalf?
3. What can you learn from Eliphaz?

CHAPTER 7

Bildad: Greatness of God

BIBLE PORTION TO READ: Job 8; 18; 25

"I WOULD RATHER play with forked lightning or take in my hands living wires than speak a reckless word against any servant of Christ, or idly repeat the slanderous darts which thousands of Christians are hurling on others, to the hurt of their own souls and bodies."

Would there be a change in your speaking and thinking if you believed and practiced these words of A. B. Simpson? How carelessly we use words! In some places in the European Alps, a mere whisper can cause a death-dealing avalanche of snow and ice. Some areas of Christian fellowship have been shattered by mere whispers of discord, gossip and despair. Take time right now to read Galatians 6:1 and Romans 14:13. First, apply them to yourself. Then remember them as you think about Bildad and his comfort to poor, suffering Job.

Bildad was a religious dogmatist who rested his conclusions upon traditions and pious platitudes. These did not help Job in his agony at the hand of

Satan or provide a solution to the problem of human suffering.

Bildad spoke to the same general theme of Eliphaz: Job was being punished because he had sinned. Bildad's particular stress, however, was the greatness of God, Who, in His greatness, has high demands. Job, according to Bildad, had fallen far short of those demands. His conclusion was wrong, but the spiritual points he developed carry important truths every believer should study.

I. Statement of God's Greatness (Job 25:1-6)

Bildad spoke three times. His first speech is chapter 8; his second, 18; and his third, 25. All of the last speech is his presentation of the greatness of God. He seemed to be summarizing what he had implied in the first two speeches: Job should have been wise enough and spiritual enough to realize God's greatness and to have a proper attitude of humility and of confession of sin.

Man, by specious self-deception, tries to convince himself that he is not so bad after all. He is better than others he could name. But in the penetrating light of God's holiness, the true and awful nature of sin is revealed; and man stands naked and depraved, stripped of all attempts to cover his sin. God rules over all. One day everyone must stand before Him to give an account. His holiness demands justice.

> But God, who is rich in mercy, for his great love wherewith he loved us, Even when we were dead in sins, hath quickened us together with Christ, (by grace ye are saved;) And hath raised us up together, and made us sit together in heavenly places in Christ Jesus: That in the ages

> **A Verse To Memorize**
> "How then can man be justified with God? or how can he be clean that is born of a woman?" (Job 25:4).

to come he might shew the exceeding riches of his grace in his kindness toward us through Christ Jesus (Eph. 2:4-7).

Bildad elaborated on the truth of God's greatness in Job 25:1-6. Two truths were given to Job (v. 2). First, God holds dominion in the world, making it necessary for man to fear Him. This is not a cringing fear that would cause one to run, but a loving reverence that brings obedience. Second, God makes peace in Heaven. A peaceful state is maintained among the angels by His authority. God is a God of peace. Though He at times ordered war in Old Testament days, and though Jesus Himself said that He "came not to send peace, but a sword" (Matt. 10:34), still God desires peace. Sin has prompted strife, and God's will is that both sin and strife cease. He cast Satan from Heaven so sin might be removed and peace maintained.

Verse 3 speaks of God's armies, meaning His heavenly hosts who inhabit Heaven, as being beyond number. The strength of kings was normally determined by the size of their armies, and Bildad used this measure to show God's greatness. Then he spoke of God's light, meaning the sunshine. Few objects of nature more clearly depict God's majesty. The sun beams on all and is universally recognized. It is essential in nature's operations, and all lives are directly dependent on it. Its life-giving rays symbolize His gracious daily influences. Its brightness suggests His glory and beauty.

Job 25:4-6 presents a contrast between God and man. It presents the implausibility of God's acceptance of man. How can man possibly stand accepted in His sight? Bildad stressed man's lowly condition by using two words for "worm" which speak of the breeding place of the worm as putrified.

Man is humiliated to think of himself as small and dependent on God; but if he is to stand before God, he must do so. The Scriptures present this truth (Isa. 57:15; Ps. 9:12; Matt. 23:12; Luke 14:11). Before a man can become a Christian, he must humble himself before God. God will not give heed to the proud, but He waits to hear the cry of the humble.

II. God Will Not Alter Justice (Job 8:2, 3; 18:4-11)

Perhaps Bildad's most cruel words were addressed to Job in his first speech (chap. 8) when he told Job he spoke like a "strong wind." He accused his distraught friend of speaking empty words and wanting to pervert God's judgment so God would think better of him than his sin deserved. Bildad reminded Job that it is impossible to alter God's judgment.

This statement was true. God is unchanged by the words of mere men, even perfect and upright men of Job's caliber. No amount of pleading can alter His basic nature or course of action. His justice demands that man live righteously before Him. It forbids the standard to be relaxed. Modernists assume that God will relax His standard and suppose He will lovingly forgive the sins of all. He cannot do

> **Daily Bible Readings**
> Sunday — God and Man Contrasted — Psalm 8
> Monday — God's Greatness — Isaiah 40:6-31
> Tuesday — God's Armies — 2 Kings 6:8-23
> Wednesday — God's Greatness — Isaiah 6:1-8
> Thursday — God's Purpose — Romans 8:28-39
> Friday — Destruction — 1 Samuel 15:1-33
> Saturday — The Righteous and Wicked — Psalm 1

this without changing His own attribute of holiness. He has provided the way of righteousness through the blood of His perfect Son, the Lord Jesus Christ. Man must take His way if he is to be accepted in God's sight. "Neither is there salvation in any other: for there is none other name under heaven given among men, whereby we must be saved" (Acts 4:12).

In his second speech, Bildad told Job that even though he tore himself in his anger, he would not be able to change anything here on earth, much less to change the powers of Heaven. He offered proof of this by telling Job several tragic results that come regularly to the wicked. Find them in Job 18:5-11.

III. God Honors Those Who Honor Him (Job 8:4-10, 20-22)

Bildad was aware of God's faithfulness to reward those who do His will. He assured Job that if he would only turn to God, God would respond favorably to him. He called upon Job to find illustrations of this truth in history. If Job would become righteous, he would be filled with laughter and joy. If he remained wicked, he would be clothed in shame.

Notice how Bildad added to Eliphaz's truth of sowing and reaping. God blesses those who follow Him; but He withholds blessing from those who do not. The general truth is correct and important to remember. But to apply it to Job's present condition was wide of the mark; for Job's suffering was not due to sin. God had presented him as perfect and upright. Job suffered from a direct attack of the evil one.

IV. Papyrus Illustration (Job 8:11-19)

A capable teacher will find good illustrations An accurate illustration verbally visualizes the message you want to get across. A poor one conveys the wrong truths and can hinder more than help. Bildad used a homely illustration to explain his ideas to Job.

Think, he said, of the papyrus (a common rush or flag that grew profusely in the Nile valley). It will begin to grow where there is little water, but unless more water comes to feed its early growth, it will soon wither and die. So, he told Job, are "all that forget God." God will cut them off just when they seem ready to do their best. He described their "trust" as a "spider's web." They are like a plant that remains green until the sun's heat strikes it, or like a plant whose roots cannot find nourishment among a heap of stones. They do not last in the heat of God's wrath. Others come along to take their place, and those who were their friends now forget them.

Do you think of one of the psalms as you read this illustration? Turn in your Bible to Psalm 1. What a contrast is offered in the experience of the righteous man! Where the dry ground papyrus of Bildad's illustration withers at its height, the water-fed tree brings forth his fruit in his season. The papyrus withers and dies, but not the tree planted by the rivers of water. Life continues vibrant and green. And "whatsoever he doeth shall prosper." The wicked man, the papyrus, is forgotten in complete disgrace. The righteous man prospers in all he does.

V. Result of Not Recognizing God's Greatness
(Job 18:12-21)

One of the most blessed benefits of salvation is the peace of God. The believer has peace, not because he is good, but because he has God. Or, more accurately, because God has him. A believer who puts his trust in the great and holy God does not need to struggle with the stresses and trials of life in his own strength. In this world, you will have tribulation; but Christ has overcome the world (John 16:33). In Him, you may have peace.

The ungodly do not have this peace. Bildad reminded Job of the awful troubles the wicked could expect:

Strength exhausted by want of food.
Destruction ready to pounce upon him.
Strength of his skin devoured.
All confidence removed.
Brimstone on his house.
His remembrance shall perish.
He shall be driven out of the world.

What a pitiful, hopeless anticipation. It is yours if you are without the cleansing blood of Christ. It is the hopeless condition of all your acquaintances who are outside the safety of salvation. Who will tell them Jesus loves them?

> God looks for an eye to see the world
>   That is dying in sin's despair.
> God looks for a hand outstretched in love
>   To lift and to show His care.
> God looks for a voice to speak in truth
>   His life-giving words of grace.
> God looks for a heart made strong through prayer
>   To cause them to seek His face.

Bildad did not realize that God's greatness goes beyond maintaining His laws. He gives special attention to his individual children. Job was His child; and though God did not lay aside His principles as set forth by Bildad in his three speeches, He dealt with Job in love. God was allowing Job to be tested for a yet more fruitful life in the days ahead. All this indicates God's great love, which goes beyond mere laws and requirements and provides the grace that gave the Redeemer for Job—and you.

What Is Your Answer?

1. What is the main theme of Bildad's discourses?

2. What effect will a recognition of God's greatness have on a person's life?

3. What attribute of God did Bildad fail to consider in trying to understand His dealings with Job?

CHAPTER 8

Zophar: Man's Dependence on God

BIBLE PORTION TO READ: Job 11; 20

EVERY CHURCH HAS its Zophar. Maybe it is just as well. He helps keep the rest of us in line. He surely must mean well because he speaks with such authority. He is a man of common sense who accepts everything in blind faith. No problems about interpretation! No reasoning! Every doubt he hears spells sin. Every difficulty of others he interprets as a sure sign of unbelief and departure from the straight and narrow. The saint called to a ministry of suffering or the unfortunate whose body or mind cannot cope with life need not expect sympathy from him. After all, does not the Word say that sin brings judgment? You are suffering? Face it! You must be sinning.

The Zophar in your church definitely has a place. He will help keep out error. He will use his common sense to bring about ready decisions in your business meetings. He will maintain the simple gospel message. Watch out, though. You might be crushed under the pressure of his sarcasm and unrelenting judgment. You probably won't be able to disagree with him, but you will want to season his spiritual purity with some spoonfuls of the sweetness of God's grace.

Fortunately, Zophar spoke last and least of the three friends. His two speeches, found in chapters 11 and 20, told Job that he suffered because he did not recognize the principle of man's dependence on God. His speeches are harsh and crude; yet, they contain truth.

I. Zophar's Severe Remarks About Job (Job 11:2-4; 20:2-5)

Zophar said Job talked too much. He was a man of a "multitude of words" and "full of talk" (literally, a "man of lips"). Even today in the Orient, much speaking is disdained. One can be judged foolish simply because he speaks too much, regardless of what he says. Zophar felt that when someone was guilty of vain speaking and mockery, others should put the person in his place and make him ashamed.

As you study the Scripture, you will see that Job had said some things he would not normally have said, things that were not right. He cursed the day of his birth, wishing he had never been born. But these expressions had risen from a heart of grief and suffering. Zophar would not allow for Job's condition. He judged solely on what Job said at this time, refusing to remember the man Job had been. It is so important in all counseling to consider the thinking and the heart attitude of the counselee. Listen with your heart! Think through the heart attitude to discover what causes the oral expression.

Job had asked for a reasonable explanation of his

> **A Verse To Memorize**
>
> "Canst thou by searching find out God? canst thou find out the Almighty unto perfection?" (Job 11:7).

suffering. He said he did not think he had sinned sufficiently to deserve all this misery. Zophar changed his words to say that Job claimed purity for himself.

With this assertion, Zophar launched into his most vicious charge, namely that Job was actually suffering less than his sin deserved. He wished that God would speak directly to Job and reveal how bad Job was. Job would discover that "secrets of wisdom" are far higher and more complicated than man's reasoning.

Then Zophar shot his arrow, "Know therefore that God exacteth of thee less than thine iniquity deserveth" (11:6). This must have hurt Job deeply. It showed him unmistakably that Zophar had little conception of what he was enduring. It proved that these friends were not entering into his experience. They did not sympathize or try to understand. They offered empty help. What more did they think he could suffer? He had lost property, family and now his health. What more was there? (His life, but God had put a hedge around that and Satan could go no farther.)

Zophar's words were true for man generally. Man who thinks he deserves good really deserves bad. He is guilty before God, and it is only of God's grace that he is not consumed. No man dares to say, "Give me my just desserts."

Think it through: If you, as a sinner, were to get what was coming to you, what would be your fate? In the light of God's Word, you would be headed for hell and destruction. No good thing would be yours.

By His infinite grace, God provides for the sinner and the saint alike many of the good things of life. Consider all the benefits of life that belong to us just because we are alive. God provides many material things—even for the sinner—but not because it is merited. If He gave to each one what was merited, no one would last a day. In addition to all the provisions of life, God has provided the most important gift for anyone who will receive it—the gift of salvation, the Lord Jesus Christ; not because it is deserved, but because of His great grace.

Zophar, as the other friends, was wrong concerning Job. Job's misery was not due to his sin. He did not deserve more misery. But even if he had sinned and did deserve more punishment, it was not Zophar's business to say it. He could not know that what he spoke was accurate. At best, it was a wild charge, and this to a man suffering excruciating pain at the hand of Satan. Zophar was a cold man with a hard, unsympathetic heart.

He went from bad to worse in his words. He inaccurately accused Job of being a hypocrite: "The triumphing of the wicked is short, and the joy of the hypocrite but for a moment" (20:5). Hypocrites come to a sad end. Their joy is only for a moment. God has no place for them. Sooner or later, they are caught in their folly.

II. Statement of Man's Dependence on God (Job 11:7-20)

This is the main theme of Zophar's speeches: man's dependence on God. God is great, man is

> **Daily Bible Readings**
>
> Sunday — Danger of the Tongue — James 3
> Monday — God Is Unsearchable — Romans 11:33-36
> Tuesday — God Is Everywhere — Psalm 139
> Wednesday — Revelation — Psalm 19
> Thursday — Hypocrites — Matthew 23:13-36
> Friday — The Two Ways — Matthew 7:13-29
> Saturday — Good and Evil — Proverbs 15

small; therefore, man is dependent on God. This was at the center of Zophar's thinking all the while. He could not refrain from making some uncomplimentary remarks about Job's character as he began his first speech, but as soon as those were out of the way, he presented his thoughts on the fact that man is dependent upon God for knowledge. "Canst thou by searching find out God? canst thou find out the Almighty unto perfection?" (11:7).

By himself man cannot know God. It is only as God chooses to reveal Himself that man can know Him. Man can investigate things on earth. In this century man has used all the remarkable talents God has bestowed to search out the hidden things of earth and space. Yet, with all the marvelous discoveries, man has not even begun to find the mysteries of God and His creation. Man cannot investigate God. He is infinite, a Spirit, dwelling in Heaven. God has revealed Himself to man through the Bible. We can know about Him, but only because He has told us what He wants us to know.

> O the depth of the riches both of the wisdom and knowledge of God! how unsearchable are his judgments, and his ways past finding out! For who hath known the mind of the Lord? or who hath been his counsellor? Or who hath first given to him, and it shall be recompensed unto him again? For of him, and through him, and to him, are all things: to whom be glory for ever. Amen (Rom. 11:33-36).

Zophar called upon the extreme measures known to man at his time to prove that God's knowledge was above man's (11:8, 9). What can be higher than Heaven, and what deeper than hell (sheol)? Or again, what is longer than earth's distances, or wider than the boundless sea? Even today, with all the travel through space, we cannot measure the boundless knowledge of our great God.

Though man cannot know God, God does know man. God can, Zophar assured Job, "cut off" man in his life and shut him up in confinement at any time. He can also "gather together" His jury to judge man. This is a figure of speech because God does His own judging. God "knoweth vain men" and sees them in their wickedness (11:11). He is not fooled by hypocrites and will not let them escape His judgment.

Apart from his assumption that Job was a hypocrite, Zophar's words were right. God does know man. Man can try all he wishes to act piously and play the hypocrite, but he cannot fool God (Prov. 15:3). God keeps the record books. We can fool others; but we can never fool God.

In view of this exact, penetrating knowledge of God, Zophar was certain Job should recognize his dependence on God and seek forgiveness for sin. If he would, God had abundant blessing for him.

Zophar used eight verses of his first speech (11:13-20) to explain these blessings to Job. Job should "prepare" his heart, "stretch out" his hands in supplication and put away "iniquity" that was in his hand. If Job did so, he would then lift up his "face without spot." He would be "stedfast" and "not fear." Having this confidence, his misery would roll away as water. Sadness would leave, and things would seem bright like a radiant morning. He would have new hope and be able to "rest in safety," without fear or shame. But Zophar warned, if Job did not do these things, he could expect that his eyes, like those of the wicked, should "fail," and he should not escape from God (v. 20). His hope would "be as the giving up of the ghost"; that is, it would die. He would have no hope.

In these thoughts, Zophar again paralleled the statements of Eliphaz and Bildad. Wonderful blessing comes to those who do right, but harm comes to those who do not. Eliphaz had strongly sounded this note with his stress on sowing and reaping, and these others simply reiterated it.

III. Dire Results When This Dependence Is Not Recognized (Job 20:6-29)

Zophar devoted all his second speech, apart from the opening verses in which he condemned Job, to the dire results for one who does not recognize his dependence on God. He developed his theme on three main thoughts.

First, such an one will perish from the earth. In 20:6 and 7 he said this would be true though the man "mount up to the heavens, and his head reach unto the clouds." In other words, self-exaltation would not help. This would be hypocritical. God would know the true feeling of his heart and he would perish. Verses 8 and 9 stress this idea, comparing the hypocrite to a dream or vision which, when one awakens, vanishes entirely.

Zophar mentioned the fate of the children of the hypocrite. They would be forced to work for the poor to restore "goods" taken unjustly in days gone by (v. 10). Though Job's children had been killed, Zophar classified him with those in this humiliating position and said that Job was no less guilty.

We do not know how long Zophar had been Job's friend. However, in 20:11 he accused Job even in his youth: "His bones are full of the sin of his youth. . . ." True, man is born a sinner, and for that reason he commits sinful acts. Here, Zophar spoke of the sin he thought had brought about Job's present suffering. He was saying that Job had been this kind of sinner from his youth. He was wrong. Job was not this kind of sinner then or later.

Second, Zophar pointed out the sweetness of sin soon passes away. He compared sin to a delicacy which one might roll in his mouth to extract all its goodness. Read 20:12-16. You will find a true and terrible picture of the subtle trickery of sin. Satan's way is so exciting, such fun, so sweet to savor— until it takes over the inner man. Then it is found to be the "gall of asps within him." Its sweetness has only been temporary. Its true nature shows up in time, and then one comes to vomit it up. Sin appeals and promises so much at first; then it leads to sad and tragic ends.

Third, Zophar listed items that take all joy from the wicked man and replace it with sorrow and remorse (20:17-29). The wicked shall not see "the rivers, the floods, the brooks of honey and butter"; that is, the good things of life. He had obtained his gain by unjust methods; so it must be returned. The wicked man shall have no inner quietness nor be able to get ahead in material savings. Rather, Zophar warned, he shall use up all his food and there will be no "goods" of any kind for others to see. When he should be prosperous, he will still be poor, and wicked persons will work against him. When he thinks he is strong, God will bring fury upon him. He will find darkness where his treasure had been; fire will consume him and his. Heaven and earth will bring judgment, likely in storm and pestilence. All his increase and goods will flow away, and he will be desolate. This, then, is the "portion of a wicked man from God, and the heritage appointed unto him by God" (v. 29).

Look at the repulsive picture. You may plunge on in your sin, somehow believing these things will not come to you. But Zophar was correct. God will not tolerate sin.

What Is Your Answer?

1. What is the main theme of Zophar's speeches?

2. Zophar's principles did not apply to Job. What lessons can you draw from this as you try to understand the sufferings of others?

3. Can peace and joy ever result when prosperity is gained by devious means? Why?

CHAPTER 9

Job Perplexed

BIBLE PORTION TO READ: Job 6:1—7:21; 9:1—10:22; 12:1—14:22; 16:1—17:16; 21; 23:1—24:25

JOB'S DAYS OF sudden, stark sorrow had passed. The effects of Satan's attack on his body, though still intense, had lost their early agony. Job had endured them all, and now he listened to the accusations of his three friends.

You have read their speeches. You have thought of their charges against the man God called perfect and upright. Each of them seemed to believe Job had grievously sinned and that he deserved all the suffering he had experienced as just punishment for wrongdoing.

Job's answer to the charges of his friends covers twenty chapters. Chapter 5 of this book, "Job's Despair" presented part of his answer. This chapter considers twelve Biblical chapters. Obviously, these cannot be treated in detail. The following chapter of this book will complete Job's answer, involving seven chapters of Job. Many truths of

Christian living will be revealed. Though Job will be seen as a perplexed individual, you will discover in him solidity and trust in God. You need to emulate him in these respects if you want to stand for God in this present evil world.

I. Remarks Concerning His Friends (Job 6; 9:2-20; 12)

Job's first reply to religious, gentlemanly Eliphaz was mainly in defense of himself and his reaction to the suffering that had befallen him. He knew Eliphaz well enough to know his words showed good judgment. Eliphaz had reason to say what he had said. Job had heard his own bitter words, and he reminded Eliphaz that he knew his words had been rash. "For the arrows of the Almighty are within me, the poison whereof drinketh up my spirit . . ." (6:4). His sorrows led him to desire death: ". . . That God would grant me the thing that I long for! Even that it would please God to destroy me . . ." (6:8, 9).

As you continue to read chapter 6, you see Job longing for pity from his friends. Instead, "My brethren have dealt deceitfully as a brook, and as the stream of brooks they pass away" (6:15). As brooks in the winter run full of ice and snow and then dry up in the summer heat, so his friends had dried up in their compassion for him (6:13-18). The right words from them might help. He had not asked them to come. He had not sought their help. "But," he asked, "what doth your arguing reprove? . . . Ye overwhelm the fatherless, and ye dig a pit for your friend" (6:25, 27).

His defense against Eliphaz, Bildad and Zophar was that they did not appreciate his great suffering.

> **A Verse To Memorize**
>
> "Though he slay me, yet will I trust in him
> ..." (Job 13:15).

They had turned against him just when he needed them most. But he would still gladly listen to them if they would speak helpful words. He was eager for godly instruction.

In chapter 12 Job assured them, "I have understanding as well as you; I am not inferior to you: yea, who knoweth not such things as these?" (v. 3). He knew the principles they presented as well as they did. He understood God's greatness and control over the world. True, Job did know them well, but not all men know them. In their hearts, men know God exists and that He is supreme (Rom. 1:19, 20); but they supress this knowledge, for it curtails their daily behavior. They give themselves over to their sinful minds.

Chapter 9 shows Job's realization of the greatness of God. It is impossible for man to be just before the holy God (vv. 2, 3). God is indeed great in works (vv. 5-9), and His ways are past finding out (vv. 10-12). Accordingly, Job knew he could not answer God; for his own mouth would condemn him (vv. 13-20). These statements implied the truths the three friends had been expounding: God is great; man is dependent; a man must sow what he reaps. Job had problems understanding the last thought, as you will see from the next passages.

II. Puzzled As to Why He Suffered (Job 7:17-21)

As you study Job 7:17-21, you will see that Job

was perplexed as to why he suffered. He mentioned it often, but two instances show his concern with greater clarity than the others. The first occurred at the close of his first reply to Eliphaz (7:17-21), where he puzzled that God would "magnify him" or give him so much attention. Since God is so great, would it not be expected that He would just overlook and pardon his sin?

Job did not speak with the wisdom or understanding he possessed. He spoke as a sinner, and so was at fault. He knew God does not overlook sin. God is just. Where sin is concerned, it is not a question of man's unimportance or the smallness of his sin. It is rather that sin is wrong and must be punished. Sin must be paid for, either by the sinner or by a substitute. Job knew this, as other verses of the book point out. In his distress, he spoke wrongly. Maybe you think that since you are not a great sinner, God will pardon your little sin. But God's holiness demands payment for sin. The glory of Christ's redemptive work is that He paid for your sin. He is your Substitute. Accept Christ as Savior, and the penalty for your sin is paid. You can have the blessed assurance Job later expressed, "I know that my redeemer liveth . . ." (19:25).

In 10:2-17 Job again spoke unwisely. As he searched for a reason for his suffering, he wondered if God simply wanted him to suffer (v. 3); if God passed inaccurate judgment upon him as mere man would do (v. 4); or if God would hunt out sin to destroy him (vv. 5, 6). Job, of course, knew none of these were true. Elsewhere you read his praises to God for being so much higher than man. His cries of perplexity show he was puzzled beyond his normal sensibilities. Can you sympathize with Job? Have

> **Daily Bible Readings**
> Sunday — Praise to God — Psalm 96
> Monday — God Made Man — Genesis 1:26, 27; 2:7-25
> Tuesday — God Controls Man — Exodus 9:13-18
> Wednesday — Wickedness — 1 Kings 21:1-16
> Thursday — Wickedness Punished — 1 Kings 21:17-26; 2 Kings 9:30-37
> Friday — Trust and Answer — 2 Chronicles 20:1-17
> Saturday — Man's Duty — Ecclesiastes 12

you wondered why things happen to you as they do? Have you always had faith to believe the wonders of Romans 8:28 and to rest in God's perfect accomplishments? It takes real faith to trust when we cannot see.

Job's puzzlement continues through verses 8-17. Since God had made him, and this so wonderfully (vv. 9-12), should he not mean much to God? Why did God not overlook his little sin? It seemed to make no difference whether he was righteous or wicked (v. 15); God hunted him like a lion (v. 16), and brought witnesses against him with increasing indignation (v. 17). What could account for his great misery? Job could not figure it out for himself, and his three friends were no help. God had not revealed the answer, and all Job could do was wonder.

Job's case was extreme; but God often lets His children experience trials of a lesser nature than his for which they can see no reason. It seems God has forgotten. But God never forgets, and circumstances never get beyond His control. He wants us to exercise faith when we cannot see the answer.

In recent months, a fine missionary family, seemingly in the midst of a successful ministry for Christ, was torn apart by the sudden death of the wife. A newborn baby lived and joined the remaining family members. The young father, having lost his wife and the mother of his three small children, still said through his tears, "The Lord is so good."

What sorrow do you have? What troubles have come your way? God knows. And God is good. Trust His everlasting love.

III. Puzzled As to Why the Wicked Do Not Suffer (Job 21:7-20; 24)

Zophar and his friends had asserted that the wicked always receive punishment. Job devoted most of two chapters to a challenge of this truth. He conceded that the wicked do have some suffering, but certainly not as much as they deserve. Read 21:7-20. The wicked do sometimes seem to be prospering in their sin. God's day of reckoning is not now. "The Lord is not slack concerning his promise, as some men count slackness; but is longsuffering to us-ward, not willing that any should perish, but that all should come to repentance" (2 Pet. 3:9). He wants all to have the opportunity to repent. But His day of judgment will come swift and sure.

In chapter 24 Job thought of all the wicked experiences that had come to him and for which no punishment had been given. Read verses 2-12. The wicked remove the landmarks and steal property from their neighbors; they steal flocks; they take the ass of the orphan and the ox of the widow; they mistreat the needy; they plunder for their food as do wild asses; they obtain their corn from the fields of others; they gather the vintage; they take clothing from those already destitute. This, said Job, made "men groan," but "yet God layeth not folly to them."

Was Job correct in his thinking? Does the principle of sowing and reaping hold true or not? The principle does hold true, but God in patience does not always call the wicked to a reckoning as soon as we believe He should. Evil men remain in power for years; gangsters go unapprehended for crime after crime; the dishonest businessman steadily grows more wealthy. Why? Because God does not work on the same timetable as man. But He knows the end from the beginning. And in His perfect time, sin will be judged. The scriptural truth is certain: what a man sows, he shall also reap.

IV. Desired To Lay His Case Before God (Job 13; 16)

Job discounted all help given to him by his friends (chaps. 13 and 16). Not only did they contribute nothing to him; he wished they would stop speaking and listen to him. He called them "miserable comforters," who had spoken only vain words (16:2, 3). If their places were reversed, he could have told them things they had told him, but he would not have been so cruel. He would, rather, have spoken words to assuage their grief. He wanted and needed comfort from them. They had sat with him on the ash heap. They had seen his suffering. But when they spoke, they only added to his great distress.

Can your friends expect comfort and help from you? Do you see in their problems a way to magnify the goodness of God? Do you help them to see His wisdom without making them feel stupid? Do you show them His strength without exaggerating their weakness? Pray with the psalmist, "Let the words of my mouth, and the meditation of my heart, be acceptable in thy sight, O LORD, my strength, and my redeemer" (Ps. 19:14). And if you cannot do this, "O that ye would altogether hold your peace!" (Job 13:5).

Job felt, too, that God was tormenting him. He said God had made him weary; God had filled his face with wrinkles; God had torn him in wrath and gnashed upon him with His teeth. The result was that Job's enemy had looked upon him, smitten him reproachfully and gathered against him. God had delivered him to the ungodly.

Was Job right in these assertions? Had God done all these things to him? Here is the basic point of Job's questioning. Does God send harm upon His children? Or is Satan responsible for all evil? The answer of the Book of Job is that Satan is responsible, but God must give the permission. God is not the author of evil. He does only good. He does not send the sickness, the accident, the sword. He does not foment war and strife. Satan does this. Satan's designs continually counter with what pleases God and benefits man. God permits him to bring his designs to pass, often using them as tests in the lives of believers. So God accomplishes good through them in spite of their evil nature.

Though Job saw God as the One Who brought all the suffering of the past dreadful days, still he looked to Him as his only Source of help. Since this was true, Job wanted to plead his case directly to God. "Also now, behold, my witness is in heaven, and my record is on high. . . . Mine eye poureth out tears unto God" (16:19, 20).

This week's memory verse, Job 13:15, gives an even stronger expression of Job's heart. Though God seemed to bring terrible calamity upon him, yet Job would not forsake Him. In fact, God could even slay him and Job would still believe God was his only help. Job 13:16-18 express Job's complete faith in God to justify him. If he could just lay his case before God, he was sure God would vindicate him.

What faith! Job had experienced the very greatest suffering; he wrongly believed God had brought it upon him; but still, he trusted wholly in God to work out justice for him. It was for Job simply to trust God until He accomplished His purpose.

What Is Your Answer?

1. How is friendship tested more severely in times of adversity than in good times?
2. Why does God let the wicked go unpunished for so long?
3. When is it most difficult to trust God?

CHAPTER 10

Reflection and Trust

BIBLE PORTION TO READ: Job 19; 26:1—31:40

A BACKWARD LOOK is often not a happy look. Fanny Crosby expressed it in these telling words:

> I don't look back; God knows the wasted effort,
> The wasted hours, the sinning and regret.
> I leave them all with Him Who blots the record,
> And then forgives; and then, in love forgets.

But for Job, with his clothes torn and his body covered with putrifying sores, a backward look reminded him of all that once had been, before all the torments of hell seemed to be unleashed on his unsuspecting person.

The contents of chapters 26 through 31 were spoken by Job after the last of the friends' speeches. Chapter 19, Job's reply to Bildad's second speech, combined with those six shows Job rising above his perplexity to a quiet reflection and beautiful expression of trust in the great and good God.

I. Memories of Former Days (Job 29:1-25; 30)

"Oh that I were as in months past, as in the days when God preserved me" (29:2). Job thought back with longing to the life he had known before his suffering had begun.

In 29:3-7 he recalled fond memories of those days. Read that passage to discover Job's blessings. In verses 8-10 he spoke of the honor he had enjoyed. Young men had accorded him honor. The aged, and even princes and nobles, stopped talking when Job stood up to speak. In verses 11-17 Job recounted times when he helped others, giving advice and counsel to the poor. He had always judged righteously in all matters. "I was eyes to the blind, and feet was I to the lame. I was a father to the poor . . ." (vv. 15, 16). People listened to him and blessed him.

Job had thought it would always be so, that men would hold him in high esteem for the rest of his days. In verses 21-25 he repeated the fact that high honor had been his. Men listened and did not speak further after he had expressed his views; indeed, they waited for him to speak, knowing that he would have the best information. Even his smile or a change in his countenance was enough to influence them. Job had been a respected person. He had not only been the richest man of the country, but his judgment and kindness exceeded all others. Job had been a great man.

What a contrast! Because people are so fickle and vacillating, they looked at their fallen hero and made fun of him. Chapter 30 presents their reaction to Job's troubles and their treatment of him after he lost his possessions. "They that are younger than I have me in derision, whose fathers I would have

> **A Verse To Memorize**
> "For I know that my redeemer liveth, and that he shall stand at the latter day upon the earth" (Job 19:25).

disdained to have set with the dogs of my flock" (v. 1).

Job described the persons who derided him in most derogatory terms through verse 8; then in verse 9 he said, "And now am I their song, yea, I am their byword." He was not talking about Eliphaz, Bildad and Zophar. They could not have been called "base men" who had been driven out of society by others. However, it was the statements of the friends that caused Job to think such things of others. Just thinking about his new reputation drove Job to the despondent tones found in verses 15 through 31. Read these verses to see a man thoroughly discouraged.

II. Job's Purity (Job 31)

In this chapter Job listed six specific areas of sin. Though his friends had not mentioned these sins by name or charged Job with them, Job felt they had implied he was guilty of them. He wished to give this clear, positive declaration of his innocence. Study each sin carefully. Can you, like Job, declare you are innocent of each one?

1. Improper relationship with a woman (vv. 1-12). Job had made a covenant with his eyes; why should he think upon a maid? In other words, he had disciplined himself in the matter of chastity. He had trained his eyes. In verse 9 he spoke even more directly. If he had permitted himself to be enticed by a woman, or had waited intentionally until the husband had departed so he could visit his neighbor's wife, then he should suffer. "For this is an heinous crime; yea, it is an iniquity to be punished by the judges" (v. 11). Job disclaimed all guilt. He recognized the seriousness and prevalence of this sin by speaking longer of it than of any other.

Adultery is a sin of the ages. In some places today it is accepted as the normal, expected way of life. Once this sin was considered so despicable it was scarcely mentioned in Christian circles. Man's sinful standards have fallen so low that even professing believers talk and joke about it (and, could it be, even participate in it?). God's laws are unchangeable. God proclaimed adultery SIN. Job knew the danger and made a covenant with his eyes. Many today need to make the same covenant. Be on guard.

2. Improper treatment of servants (vv. 13-15). When Job's workers complained to him, he listened to them. He recognized that God had made all men equal, so all have the same rights. Also, if Job did not treat them justly, he would have to answer to God. Masters and servants, employers and employees all come into view here. There should be mutual respect on the part of both parties. The master is to give proper pay and benefits; the servant is to render good service.

3. Improper treatment of the poor, the widow and the orphan (vv. 16-23). Job listed all the ways he might have sinned against these less fortunate ones. He knew what the sins were, but he was certain he had not been guilty.

> **Daily Bible Readings**
> Sunday — The Needy — Amos 5:11-15; 6:1-7
> Monday — Love of Money — Luke 18:18-27
> Tuesday — Love — 1 Corinthians 13
> Wednesday — Wisdom — 1 Corinthians 1:18-25
> Thursday — Wisdom — Proverbs 9
> Friday — Kinsman-Redeemer — Ruth 4:1-14
> Saturday — Resurrection — 1 Thessalonians 4:13—5:11

Scripture makes it clear that God notices how we treat the poor and underprivileged. The prophets spoke often of this sin (e.g., Amos 2:7; 5:11; 6:4-6; 8:4, 5).

4. Idolatry (vv. 24-28). In verses 24 and 25 the god mentioned was money. Job denied that his wealth had been his hope and confidence. He continued in verses 26 and 27 that neither had the sun or moon been his god. In his day, and still in many parts of the earth, these creations of God are worshiped as the source of life, fertility and growth. But Job worshiped the true God. In verse 28 he made clear how wrong he would have been to deny "the God that is above."

An idol is anything considered more important than the true God. Think through your desires and delights. Do you have some idols? How easy it is to make people, money, pleasure, sports, fame or success a god, and so deny the true God of Heaven.

5. Improper relationships with fellowmen (vv. 29-32). Job called upon his own servants to testify that no stranger had ever been turned away from his door without food and shelter. This was a special problem in days gone by. There were no motels or restaurants. The only resource available to a stranger was a generous and hospitable "open door." Job had provided this to all who asked.

Circumstances today change the situation, but the principle of proper respect and treatment of other people must still be observed if we are to please God. Be ready to extend hospitality whenever the need arises.

6. Improper use of land (vv. 38-40). Job declared he had not been unjust in his farming practices, whether to the owner of the land he worked or to the servants who worked it. He had not defrauded anyone in his farming. This declaration covered most of his business relationships.

It is easy to excuse dishonesty as shrewd business methods. You may be able to rationalize in your mind, but you cannot fool God.

III. The Lot of the Wicked (Job 27:8-23)

Job, in other chapters, challenged his three friends in their contention that the wicked always suffer. However, as you read 27:8-23, you find that Job, in this closing speech, made certain he was in basic agreement with them after all. Perhaps as he talked, his mind cleared and he separated their accusations to him personally from the true principle they presented. He did not admit personal wickedness, but he did assert that the wicked do suffer for their sin.

In verse 8 Job observed that whatever a man may

have gained in life he will lose at death. Also, when the wicked man cries out for help, God will not hear him (vv. 9, 10). In verse 14 Job began to show how completely undesirable the lot of the wicked is. His children are born only to die by the sword; they do not have enough to eat; his descendants will be buried without benefit of weeping widows (without mourning).

All Job said sounds very much like the speeches of his friends. Except for one thing! Job did not admit that his suffering was caused by wickedness. Instead he maintained, "My righteousness I hold fast, and will not let it go: my heart shall not reproach me so long as I live" (v. 6).

IV. Wisdom Found Only in God (Job 28)

As you read Job's words, study his beautiful, poetic manner of speaking. It is especially noticeable in chapter 28.

In verses 1-11 Job revealed where man's best efforts in wise activity could be found—in earthly endeavors. He told of mining operations where man digs for gold, iron and brass, penetrating deep into the earth to find them and to bring them to the surface for use. Man's knowledge in these areas sets him far above the knowledge of fowl, vultures or lions (vv. 7, 8). Also, man had done quite remarkable feats, said Job, in digging away mountains, cutting channels for water supply and building dams for flood control. One who carefully studies history will soon come to the conclusion that, though men of this century have captured the atom and explored space, men who went before showed superb earthly knowledge.

But with all that man had done, he had not yet discovered the source of true wisdom. True wisdom is not to be found in man-made activities.

True wisdom is found only in God, Who sees all the earth and controls all nature. He is the One Who gave "weight" (force) to the wind. He measured out the water to its appointed places. It is for man to fear the Lord and depart from evil. In his terrible suffering experience, Job must simply trust that God in His wisdom knew the answer.

We find a wonderful truth in Job's words. We think ourselves to be wise. Great monuments of science and accomplishment prove the fact. But still, we do not have true wisdom. Actually, many of man's accomplishments have only made more problems for mankind, problems that he cannot resolve with his finite mind. True wisdom is found only in God (Ps. 111:10).

V. The Redeemer Expected (Job 19:25-27)

The highest note of hope and trust reached by Job is found in chapter 19, his answer to Bildad's second series of rebukes. The well-known text (19:25-27) concerned his hope of the Redeemer Who would come. Job was despondent as he began the response to Bildad, saying that his friends, his kinfolk, his servants and even his wife had failed him. He cried out, "Why do ye persecute me as God, and are not satisfied with my flesh? Oh that my words were now written! oh that they were printed in a book!" (vv. 22, 23).

Then he spoke words that have blessed all believers who have heard them: "For I know that my redeemer liveth, and that he shall stand at the latter day upon the earth" (v. 25).

The particular meaning of "redeemer" in Job's day was of a next of kin who would ransom or avenge one who had fallen into debt or bondage or the position of a slayer. (You may remember the experience of Ruth and Boaz in the book bearing her name.) Job saw his Redeemer as his Avenger before those who had wronged him. He also saw Him standing on the earth, as it were, face to face with his present accusers, to vindicate him from their false charges. The words *latter day* are literally "afterwards." Sometime after he died, the Redeemer would vindicate him.

Verses 26 and 27 speak of Job's own resurrection as a time when he would personally see God. Job identified God with the Redeemer. His statements show he believed the Redeemer would be on the earth for him to see after his resurrection. Job saw this One Who would vindicate him here on earth as the Messiah, God Himself.

Job spoke from a sorry state: no family, no possessions or friends, sick of body and ready to die. Yet he had all the hope a man needed! He knew his Redeemer lived and he would see God, Who would make all things right.

Friend, do you know the comfort of the future resurrection?

> For the Lord himself shall descend from heaven with a shout, with the voice of the archangel, and with the trump of God: and the dead in Christ shall rise first: Then we which are alive and remain shall be caught up together with them in the clouds to meet the Lord in the air: and so shall we ever be with the Lord. Wherefore comfort one another with these words" (1 Thess. 4:16-18).

Our Kinsman-Redeemer—He Who has paid for

our redemption with His own precious blood—will receive every believer to Himself. Satan, the accuser, will no longer have power over us to lead us to defeat. We shall be with the Lord for ever and ever. Take comfort in this glorious hope!

> Lift up your heads, pilgrims aweary!
> See day's approach now crimson the sky;
> Night shadows flee, and your Beloved,
> Awaited with longing, at last draweth nigh.
>
> Even so, come, precious Lord Jesus!
> Creation waits redemption to see;
> Caught up in clouds, soon we shall meet Thee—
> O blessed assurance, forever with Thee!
>
> *Mabel Johnston Camp*

What Is Your Answer?

1. What sin is the most serious in God's sight?
2. What characteristic makes a man truly wise?
3. What Messianic prophecy is found in today's Scripture?
4. Do you have the blessed hope of the resurrection?

CHAPTER 11

Elihu Speaks

BIBLE PORTION TO READ: Job 32:1—37:24

JOB, THE SUFFERER, had listened to the condemnations of his friends. Now, in utter despair, he cried out, "Oh that one would hear me! behold, my desire is, that the Almighty would answer me . . ." (Job 31:35).

Sitting nearby, listening to every word of the many speeches that had sounded upon the air, was an intelligent, well-mannered, young man. The more he heard, the more distraught he became. As each friend spoke, he must have lifted his hands in disgust, held his lips to keep the sneer from showing, and done all else that an angry young man would do in the face of stupid remarks from his elders.

Finally, he could contain his aggravation no longer. He was angry at Job because he justified himself, rather than God. He was angry at the friends because all their words had failed to answer Job, only condemn him. In his anger he said, in words like these, "I am young, and you are very old; wherefore I did not show you my opinion. You should be able to say wise things because you are older. But great men are not always wise and do not always understand judgment. None of you could answer poor Job. Therefore, listen to me while I show you my opinion."

The angry young man was Elihu, the son of Barachel, the Buzite. It took him the space of six chapters to give his reasons for speaking and then to speak. In the first five verses of chapter 32, Elihu said four times that "his wrath was kindled." It was apparent he could hardly wait to tell those gathered at the ash heap what he thought were the answers to Job's distress.

I. Elihu's Reasons for Speaking (Job 32)

Elihu presented a twofold motivation for his speaking: (1) he desired to rebuke Job for trying to justify himself; (2) he wanted to give answers to Job's questions that would be wiser and more to the point than the answers given by the friends.

Elihu used all of chapter 32 preparing to say what he wanted to say. As you read it, you will discover he wanted very much to speak earlier; but he had refrained, giving opportunity for the older men to finish all they had to say. In verse 6 he spoke with modesty, but as he continued, he left his modest approach to show the others their errors.

Elihu was not truly modest, but proud. As the others talked, he kept quiet; but he chafed at the restriction, waiting only because they were older. He knew what he had to say would be far superior, and he could not wait to display his better knowledge. Take a lesson from him. Avoid false modesty. Usually, people are not fooled. Surely God is not. He looks on the heart. He looks for true humility.

> **A Verse To Memorize**
>
> "The spirit of God hath made me, and the breath of the Almighty hath given me life" (Job 33:4).

II. Why Did Job Suffer? (Job 33)

Elihu was so eager to speak that he was like a bottle of new wine, ready to burst (32:18, 19). He reminded the listeners that his words would come from the uprightness of his heart. He was, he claimed, standing in God's stead (33:6). He would speak for God regarding the reason for Job's suffering. Job should listen.

First, God, because of His greatness, is not required to give an account for His actions (vv. 12, 13). Job's desire for God to do this was wrong. Instead, Job and all men should trust God through every circumstance of life. God is supreme and absolute; man is finite. God is holy and just; man is sinful. God in His greatness can do what He wishes to do. Elihu spoke wisely.

Next, Elihu identified two ways in which God speaks to man (vv. 14-22). Perhaps if Job realized these, he would know why God was dealing with him as He was. First, God speaks by divine revelation which may come once or twice by dream or vision, but which is often not understood by the person who receives it. In Old Testament days the revelation of God was given to individuals. God made His mind known to saints of old like Noah and Abraham, and even to some who were not saints, such as Laban (Gen. 20:3; 31:24).

Now God speaks to us through the written Word.

Read 2 Timothy 3:16. He wants us to read it and obey. He has given it to us as a lamp and a light to guide us in the path He has planned. If you find it difficult to walk for Him, check up on the amount of time you spend reading His map for your life.

God also speaks, according to Elihu, by sending chastening such as Job was experiencing. The other friends had not presented this possibility to Job. They had thought of suffering only as an expression of punishment for sin; but Elihu depicted the awful suffering experience as a means of God's revelation, parallel with dreams and visions. Elihu wanted Job to realize that God might be trying to tell him something through his agony. If Job would listen and learn, God would return him to a place of blessing. God's desire, insisted Elihu, was to be gracious to Job and to deliver him from going down to the pit (v. 24). Look at the blessings listed in verses 25 and 26. These would follow if Job would accept the correction and turn to God.

In verses 27-30 Elihu summarized his whole thought. When a man confesses his sin, God delivers his soul.

Was Elihu correct in his statements? Factually, of course, he was. God will hear and deliver anyone who calls upon Him. He offers full forgiveness to the one who asks in faith believing, whether a sinner or a saint.

Elihu's belief that suffering is used by God as a means of chastening and correction was also accurate. God does send chastening and correction to bring man to Him. The other friends had said that suffering was only a means of punishment. But Elihu saw this further possibility.

> **Daily Bible Readings**
> Sunday — Chastening — Hebrews 12:1-13
> Monday — Blessing — Psalm 94:1-12
> Tuesday — Do Not Boast! —
>   Proverbs 27:1-11
> Wednesday — Foolish Boasting — Isaiah
>   10:5-19
> Thursday — Vain and True Prayer —
>   Matthew 6:1-15
> Friday — God's Greatness — Exodus
>   14:13-31
> Saturday — God's Greatness — Joshua
>   10:7-14

It is God's plan for parents to correct and chasten their children. Read Hebrews 12:6-11. God, our Heavenly Father, does the same for His own. When God sends chastening and correction, profit from it. Learn the lesson He wants to teach you.

Elihu assumed Job had sinned and needed God's correction. This was not so. He proved to be just as wrong in his evaluation of Job as Eliphaz, Bildad and Zophar had been.

Elihu was to be commended in his attitude toward the poor man who sat on the ash heap. He showed his sympathy, refraining from the sarcasm that had characterized the others. He even said, "I desire to justify thee" (v. 32). He meant that he wished to judge Job fairly and give him every opportunity to vindicate himself.

When you counsel or advise others, do it with tenderness and sympathetic care. Put yourself in the other's place. Remember that sometimes saying nothing is better than saying the wrong thing.

III. God Is Not Unjust (Job 34)

In chapter 34 Elihu turned from speaking to Job to address the three friends. They must have wondered what this brash young man had in mind to challenge their wisdom and understanding. He did not make them wait long for their answer. He began at once to rebuke them and to give them what he considered to be the true answers to why the righteous suffer. However, he softened his rebuke by calling upon their wisdom to judge what he was about to say.

As you study 34:10-30, you will discover several points Elihu used to express his feelings. They may be summarized in this way: God is great and can do no wrong; man must not question His divine actions; God knows that no sinner is overlooked for punishment; this punishment may come in a variety of ways. His thinking was true, but he hardly said anything different. The others had already said much the same. They, too, had exalted God. They had warned Job not to think God could err in judgment.

Perhaps as you have studied the words of Elihu, God has spoken through His Word to show you some area of your life that needs forgiveness and cleansing. Pray to God, as Elihu suggested to Job. You will find Him waiting in love to show you His favor. Read Ephesians 2:4-10 for added strength to live for Him.

Elihu turned from the three friends to speak again to Job (vv. 31-37). Elihu urged him to profit from all he had heard. He should admit that the chastisement had come from God and promise to cease from offending God's holiness. He should ask God to teach him what his sin had been so he would sin no more.

Elihu had promised when he began to speak that he would say wiser things than the others. Learn a lesson from him. He promised more than he was able to deliver. He boasted that what he would say would solve Job's problems. He thought he could do more than he was able to do. Never boastfully promise to do more than you are able to do. God is not pleased with empty, prideful words. Yet, it is easy for the average person, under stress or wanting to impress, to claim more knowledge or wisdom than he has. Avoid this trap of Satan.

IV. Why Do the Righteous Suffer As Well As the Wicked? (Job 35)

Again speaking to Job, Elihu continued to talk about the suffering of the righteous (35:1-12). He condemned Job for thinking he did not deserve what God was doing to him. Because of God's greatness, He is not influenced by the acts of men. They will not change His judgments. In fact, Elihu believed the righteous do not suffer and Job was wrong in believing they do. If God punished the righteous, Elihu believed He would then be unjust. God is perfect justice so this is impossible, Elihu seemed to say.

"Surely," Elihu continued to tell Job, "God will not hear vanity" (35:13). Perhaps Job had been praying in the wrong way. God would not hear one who prayed vainly. If God did not seem to respond to his cries, probably Job was not praying as he should.

Again we hear the remedy recommended by the

other friends. If Job would simply repent before God, submit to His will and pray as he should, God would hear. In general, Elihu gave good advice. Men should repent. They should submit to God's will. They should follow His pattern for true prayer. When they do, God will hear and answer in great and mighty ways (Jer. 33:3).

V. God Is Great; Therefore Man Must Submit (Job 36:1—37:24)

In all Elihu said, good things though they were, he missed the mark in advising Job. As he continued for what amounted to two chapters more, he spoke on the theme of the greatness of God. His statements in these chapters may be divided into two areas where God's greatness is seen: (1) in His dealings with men (36:1-21); (2) in His execution of nature (36:22—37:24).

In four simple words, Elihu swept away Job's suspicion that God was unjust: "Behold, God is mighty" (36:5). Elihu showed God's just dealings with men. He gave evidence of God's glorious creation. Then he concluded: ". . . The Almighty . . . is excellent in power, and in judgment, and in plenty of justice: he will not afflict. Men do therefore fear him: he respecteth not any that are wise of heart" (37:23, 24). Surely Elihu sought to impress Job with God's greatness.

He is to be commended for this. Haven't you been blessed to think about the great God you serve? But Elihu was saying nothing new. Job himself had extolled God's greatness. The three friends had spoken at length about it. And Elihu had elaborated in ways that seemed right to him.

The emphasis on God's greatness is sorely

needed in our world and in our churches. Man exalts himself, and many have come to believe they need no one else. God is left out entirely in their thinking. The current theory is that every man can decide his course by himself. With the superior knowledge of this enlightened age, who needs a Supreme Being? Even the average church member seems to have little concept of the great God and His justice. Ask yourself these questions:

1. How long has it been since I carefully reviewed my daily living in the light of God's righteousness?
2. How much time do I spend in effectual, fervent prayer each day? Each week?
3. Is God in control of every area of my life?
4. Can I call to mind current blessings from His good hand?
5. Do I love Him more today than ever before?

God wants people who are submitted completely and unreservedly to His will. In the time of judgment, all persons will "bow . . . and . . . confess that Jesus Christ is Lord, to the glory of God the Father" (Phil. 2:10, 11). But then there will be no time for reward. How much better to bow now before the Lord of glory and be prepared for an abundant entrance into Heaven! Will you bow before Him today?

What Is Your Answer?

1. How do you compare Elihu's character with the three friends?
2. What contributions in thought did Elihu make that were not made by the three friends?
3. How would you compare Elihu's feeling toward Job with the others?

CHAPTER 12

God Himself Speaks

BIBLE PORTION TO READ: Job 38:1—41:34

WHEN GOD SPEAKS, the high mountains tremble;
When God speaks, the loud billows roll;
When God speaks, my heart falls to list'ning,
And there is response in my soul.

Carlton C. Buck

"Then the LORD answered Job out of the whirlwind, and said" (38:1). Four men had used all their wisdom and knowledge to try to explain to Job the reasons for his great suffering. As they spoke, Job had asked God to speak to him (13:22-24). Now God spoke, but hardly in the way Job expected.

God prepared Job for His words by saying: "Gird up now thy loins like a man: for I will demand of thee, and answer thou me" (38:3). This brings to mind Paul's words to the Corinthians: "Watch ye, stand fast in the faith, quit you like men, be strong" (1 Cor. 16:13). God was preparing Job for the hard lessons he was going to learn.

God used questions about nature to show Job he was not as wise as he thought. If Job was not able to understand simple facts of nature, how could he enter into the secret counsels of God? Look at two general observations regarding the things God said; then consider the method God used to impress upon Job his incompetency.

I. General Observations

One of the great lessons of the Book of Job is that man is unable to solve his own problems; he requires revelation from God. Job and his friends had many ideas about the fact of suffering—Job's suffering in particular—but none had come up with the correct answer to the question, "Why do the righteous suffer?" The question was beyond their human understanding. If there was to be an answer, God must speak. And God spoke!

How thankful we should be for God's Word! The inadequacy of Job and the friends is symbolic of the inadequacy of all men. Without God's revelation, we would be in complete ignorance about Him, His love and mercy, the impending danger of eternal punishment and His wonderful plan of salvation. There would be no church, no prayer, no fellowship of Christians, no hope of Heaven. But God has revealed these sacred truths. The Bible is indeed a treasure worth everything! Have you learned the simple, yet blessed, children's chorus?

> I have a wonderful treasure,
> The gift of God without measure,
> And so we travel together,
> My Bible and I.

Do you read your Bible and obey its truths? Or is it a closed book, gathering dust from disuse?

Because of the emotional involvement of Job and

> **A Verse To Memorize**
>
> "Then the LORD answered Job out of the whirlwind, and said" (Job 38:1).

his friends, they were not able to find answers as well as they might have under other circumstances. As they talked, they became angry with one another. Had they kept their tempers, they might have moved nearer the truth. For this reason, as well as their ignorance, it was necessary for God to speak.

Persons who are emotionally involved seldom speak well on any issue. Their thinking is warped. They do not evaluate objectively. They refuse to consider all the facts. Good decisions call for cool, clear heads. Read Philippians 4:4-7.

As you consider God's message to Job, consider what He did not say. The basic question of the book has been, "Why do the righteous suffer?" Surprisingly, God did not answer this. In fact, He did not speak of Job's suffering at all. He knew about it, of course. He had allowed it. Also, you can be certain He knew the answer. He knows all things. The deliberate omission must mean God knew it was better for Job to trust simply on the basis of his love for God. Trust is greater when one does not see the reason for adverse circumstances. God wanted Job to have this kind of deep, abiding faith. He wants that for you too.

God began to speak in much the same vein as the others. He stressed His greatness and man's smallness. A contrast began to appear, however. When the others spoke, no one was brought to repentance or a change in thinking. When God spoke, Job repented twice; once, in the middle of God's speaking (40:3-5), and again at the close (42:1-6). Two factors made the difference.

First, God Himself was speaking. Job might be able to discount much that the friends said; but when God spoke, Job knew he must listen. God's authority was final. Second, God used a different approach. The human participants simply stated that God is great and talked of the great things He does. But God asked Job questions he could not answer. This showed Job very forcibly his own incompetency.

God knows how to deal with His children. He knows what will penetrate hard hearts and bring repentance. Jesus knew how to talk to the Jewish ruler who came to Him by night. He met Nicodemus where he was (John 3). He also knew how to work with the sinful Samaritan woman (John 4). He brought her to Himself with questions that pierced her heart, causing her to believe and to become a bright witness for the Savior. His approach was entirely different with each, but His way was effective and brought repentance. Sometimes God speaks harshly; sometimes, in tenderness. Have ears eager to hear and a soul ready to respond when He speaks.

II. Man's Incompetency in Explaining Nature (Job 38)

This great section begins simply, "Then the LORD answered Job out of the whirlwind." This is the only place in Scripture that God spoke in this manner for such an extended length of time. God showed unusual interest in this occasion.

Evidently His voice was audible both to Job and

> **Daily Bible Readings**
> Sunday — Creation — Genesis 1
> Monday — Creation — John 1:1-3; Colossians 1:15-17
> Tuesday — Creation Cursed — Genesis 3:8-19
> Wednesday — Natural Revelation — Psalm 19:1-6
> Thursday — Special Revelation — Psalm 19:7-14
> Friday — Revelation in Christ — Hebrews 1:1-3
> Saturday — Value of Revelation — 2 Timothy 3:10-17

to his friends. In fact, the friends were addressed in 42:7 and 8. The voice came from the whirlwind. Apparently, then, there was no visible appearance, only the voice of God. He spoke visibly in the Angel of the Lord to Abraham (Gen. 18) and in the Captain of the host to Joshua (Josh. 5:13—6:5); but it is not likely He did so here.

God's questions to Job involved various aspects of nature. Did Job know basic facts about the earth's creation; setting the bounds of the sea; establishment of days; the source of seawater; the mystery of death; the breadth of the earth; the formation of snow and hail; the reason for lightning, storm and rain; the place of the stars?

Where was Job, God asked, when creation occurred (38:4)? This reminded Job that he was only temporal, while God is eternal. In verse 5 God asked Job Who made the earth, a reminder that God

Himself had done so. And in verse 6 God asked Job about the foundations of the earth, to remind him how wonderfully the earth was made. It had no foundation, so the One Who made it had to be far superior to man.

If Job would take time to look at God's great creation, he would know without a doubt the true greatness of God. Nature could teach him this truth. The small, inquisitive child, bending to the earth to study a crawling ant, ladened down with a crumb it is carrying home for its supper, studies nature. You and I would do well to look at the wonders created by our mighty and great God. Never become so familiar with the blazing sunrise, the flashing lightning, the food you eat, the air you breathe, that you forget God's glory revealed in them. Our great God has wonderfully spoken through His book of nature as well as through His Word of special revelation.

III. Man's Incompetency in Regard to Animals
(Job 39)

God directed questions about animals to Job in chapter 39. As you read the chapter, you find God talking about the wild goat, the wild ass, the unicorn, the ostrich, the horse, the hawk and the eagle. Probably Job thought he knew the habits of these animals. But again, as God spoke, Job realized he knew little.

Look at some interesting facts about these animals. All animals give evidence of God's abundant provision. See 39:1-4 for a picture of the life span of animals and God's care for them.

Concerning the wild goats, did Job know their habits, since they lived in lofty mountain rocks? Did he know when they bore their young, how long their gestation periods were? Probably he did not.

Verses 5-8 tell about the wild ass. This animal lives in the wilderness. Did Job know who had set it free to roam? God wanted to impress Job that these animals were all under God's protective care. The wild goat and the wild ass, as well as God's other animals, were created for a special purpose. God had a reason for making each one as He did.

Among the animals God mentioned is the unicorn (39:10-12). This animal has been likened to the buffalo because of its mighty head and shoulder strength. It was not to be harnessed to a plow; it was untamable. Yet it was controlled by God and fulfilled His purpose.

God, in His great wisdom, knew how to make you for the purpose He had planned. He has made man to work, to think, to produce. He created each of us with the ability to perform what He planned.

IV. Reproof of Job (Job 40:1-14)

After showing Job his inadequacy to explain everyday matters in nature, God gave him opportunity to speak. Job had requested the privilege, but after hearing God speak, he knew his words were nothing. His only reply was, "Behold, I am vile; what shall I answer thee? I will lay mine hand upon my mouth" (40:4). Job had been brought face to face with his smallness in contrast to God's greatness. He had no words left within him.

This is the reaction when a person meets God. He has a closed mouth and realizes his own unworthiness. Isaiah was a great prophet, outstanding for courage and righteousness. But when he saw the Lord high and lifted up in the temple, he cried out, "Woe is me! for I am undone; because I am a man of unclean lips . . ." (Isa. 6:5).

A true meeting with God does not result in a brash, exuberant show. It results in that person falling on his face before God in confession of sin and worship of God. The outward expression may come later; but quiet confession is first.

After Job confessed, God told him the qualifications he should possess if he were to lay his case before God as he had requested to do. In substance, these qualifications were: be as strong as God; be able to thunder in the heavens; be decked with the same majesty, excellency, glory and beauty as God; be able to control others by wrath, and humble the proud; and be able to tread down the wicked into the dust of the earth. Job could not do these things. Accordingly, it was fitting and necessary that he stay in his rightful, humble place and not seek to contend with the Lord of the universe. How foolish of Job to have tried! But man can be extremely foolish. None of us is immune.

V. Man's Incompetency in Regard to Behemoth and Leviathan (Job 40:15—41:34)

God chose Job's pride as the way to bring him to repentance. Job was a fine man, full of good things for which God could praise him. But God wanted to conquer Job's pride. Pride is one of the most common sins, even among believers. God's Word has many references to the evils of pride and the results of its presence in our lives. As you think about Job, determine to accept God's help to make and keep you His humble servant. Then you will be useful for His glory.

Job 40:15 (and following) describe an animal called "behemoth." As nearly as can be determined, this was the hippopotamus, known in Egypt and inhabiting the river, as suggested in verse 21.

The description of this animal was used to bring proud Job's attention to the great Creator of this creature. Job should consider carefully before contending with the God Who could create and control such a beast.

Chapter 41 describes the animal called "leviathan," commonly identified with the crocodile. This was also well-known in Egypt and inhabited the river. Verses 1-9 show that man cannot control this creature. Since no man is able to stand before this animal, certainly no one can stand before the God Who made it (vv. 10, 11). Verses 12-34 give a detailed description of this beast, "a king over all the children of pride" (v. 34).

As you read about these two strange creatures, you may wonder why God devoted so much time to them. We cannot know the reason, but one thing is certain. The God Who could create and control these animals, great and mighty as they were, is the God before Whom Job—and you—must bow. Bow before Him now for salvation, and in a future day you will be able to stand before His presence with great joy (Jude 24).

What Is Your Answer?

1. What can a person learn about God from nature?

2. Why does a close walk with God cause one to see his own sinfulness?

CHAPTER 13

Job Rewarded

BIBLE PORTION TO READ: Job 42

THERE WAS A man in the land of Uz, whose name was Job. . . .

Now there was a day when the sons of God came to present themselves before the LORD, and Satan came also among them.

And the LORD said unto Satan, Hast thou considered my servant Job, that there is none like him in the earth, a perfect and an upright man, one that feareth God, and escheweth evil?

Then Satan answered the LORD, and said, Doth Job fear God for nought?

But put forth thine hand now, and touch all that he hath, and he will curse thee to thy face.

And the LORD said unto Satan, Behold, all that he hath is in thy power; only upon himself put not forth thine hand. . . .

Again there was a day when the sons of God came to present themselves before the LORD. . . .

And the LORD said unto Satan, Hast thou considered my servant Job? . . . still he holdeth fast his integrity, although thou movedst me against him, to destroy him without cause.

And Satan answered the LORD . . . Put forth

> thine hand now, and touch his bone and his flesh, and he will curse thee to thy face.
>
> And the LORD said unto Satan, Behold, he is in thine hand; but save his life (Job 1:1, 6-12; 2:1-6).

You have traveled with Job through this troubled time in his life. You have seen him sitting on the ash heap, scraping himself with broken pieces of pottery. You have heard his friends try to comfort him, but in their human frailty bring him more distress. You have seen Job listening and answering. You have seen him sink to the depths of despair and cry out for an opportunity to ask God why.

But you have not heard Job curse God. Satan had failed. His attacks on God's perfect and upright man ended in defeat—just as God knew they would.

Job still did not know why. Then God spoke. God did not answer Job's questions. Instead, He gave further evidences of His greatness. All Job's questions were lost as he said:

> I know that thou canst do every thing. . . . I have heard of thee by the hearing of the ear: but now mine eye seeth thee. Wherefore I abhor myself, and repent in dust and ashes (42:2, 5, 6).

I. Job Repented (Job 42:1-6)

Job's repentance showed a changed viewpoint and a humble heart. In all he said, Job had acknowledged God's greatness and wisdom; but now he realized in a new and vital way that the One he served was the omnipotent, all-knowing God.

Before he had wanted to speak to God to present his case and demand an answer. Now he wanted to ask God to instruct him. He stood with closed mouth to hear the words of his God.

> **A Verse To Memorize**
>
> "So the LORD blessed the latter end of Job more than his beginning . . ." (Job 42:12).

Job's repentance was genuine, not halfhearted. He abhorred himself and recognized he was a sinner. He had defended himself against such charges by his friends; now he had heard God, and he readily admitted his sin.

Find here a test for your own spirituality. When Job became acutely aware of God's reality, he abhorred himself and his goodness. This is a normal result for anyone who lives close to God. (See Isaiah 6 and Romans 7.) Ask yourself, "How much do I abhor my sinfulness before God?"

II. God and the Three Friends (Job 42:7-9)

God's wrath was kindled against Eliphaz, Bildad and Zophar. He was displeased; therefore, they were in line for punishment unless something was done to alleviate His displeasure. They had not spoken of God "the thing that is right," as Job had. God vindicated Job. He had insisted his suffering was not because of sin, while the friends had said it was. God now said Job was right. This does not mean God approved of everything Job had said (38:2). Nor had everything the friends said been wrong. God's statement must be taken comparatively. In general, what the friends said was not as correct as what Job said. He was closer to the truth about God and the reason for his suffering. Also, Job spoke from a vexed heart caused by his suffering, while the friends spoke from proud self-righteousness. God noted the circumstances and judged guilt accordingly.

Job was further vindicated when God prescribed the punishment. The three friends were to go to Job with seven bullocks and seven rams, offer them as sacrifices and intercede with Job to pray for them; for God would accept Job. This meant the friends must completely reverse their behavior. During their speeches, Job had been judged guilty, and they were the judges. Now he was approved of God, and they must seek his help. He was not the sinner; they were the sinners. He was not in line for God's punishment; they were. God told them to go to Job, seek his favor and ask for help.

This was humiliating. Would Job intercede for them so God would forgive them of their sin? God has His own way of making things right. They had not been sympathetic with Job. They had been mean, not really wanting to help him, but rather to take advantage of his suffering condition. Now God rectified the situation. They must go to Job in humility. God knows the hearts of all. He knows the righteous; and when they are called upon to suffer, God in due time brings vindication. Those who take advantage of them meanwhile must answer to Him.

Before Job prayed for his friends they were to bring sacrifices. Notice the truth here. The sacrifices prescribed by God in the Old Testament prefigured the great coming Sacrifice, the Lord Jesus Christ. The animals could not atone for sin, but they pointed ahead to Him Who could and would offer Himself as the atonement for sin. When Christ died on the cross, He made atonement available, not only for all who should live after Him, but

> **Daily Bible Readings**
>
> Sunday — Incomplete Repentance — Matthew 27:3-10
> Monday — Confession — 1 John 1:1-10
> Tuesday — Empty Sacrifice — Isaiah 1:11-18; Amos 5:21-24
> Wednesday — Sure Salvation — John 10:22-30
> Thursday — The Daughters' Inheritance — Numbers 27:1-11
> Friday — Trust in God — 1 Samuel 17:31-51
> Saturday — Trust in God — Proverbs 3:1-13

for all who had lived and believed before as well.

Accordingly, these men were to come for forgiveness only after prefiguring Christ's death in their place. An earlier chapter stated that the men were doubtless regenerated men. Hence, they were to come to Job with sacrifices not for salvation, but for restoration of fellowship. They had sinned, and fellowship needed to be restored. In your daily Bible readings you have read 1 John 1:9. They needed to come for forgiveness—and so do you when you sin. Fellowship is restored to the believing sinner on the basis of Christ's atonement, just as salvation was given when first you believed.

These sacrifices alone were not adequate. Intercessory prayer was necessary. The Israelite sacrifices were never sufficient in themselves. They were empty formalism without faith and prayer. God indicted Israel for this (cf. Amos 5:21-27; Isa. 1:11ff.). We, too, must avoid empty formalism in our church activities. What do you think about during the Lord's Supper? What is your attitude during a baptismal service? How long has it been since you truly worshiped God in the worship service?

What if the friends had come to Job for forgiveness and he had turned his back and walked away? It would be hard for them to ask his forgiveness, but perhaps it would be more difficult for him to respond to their request. They had hurt him when he needed help. God does not always indicate an easy way. He wanted Job to be willing to forgive and even to intercede for them. You and I, too, must be willing to forgive those who despitefully use us.

III. Blessing to Job (Job 42:10-17)

When Job granted forgiveness to his friends at God's command, he had completed his test. He had proved faithful all through his testing experience. He had not cursed God as Satan had predicted. Job's reward had been assured; now blessing was possible.

First, the relatives came forward—as they should have done before—to eat, comfort and give him money and gold. Where had these people been when Job's suffering had begun? Perhaps they, too, had thought Job guilty and suffering punishment from God. Now they had heard of his vindication. We may believe Job appreciated their coming, even though it was late. It showed that he had been accepted. He had missed their presence (19:13, 14).

These relatives had been fair-weather friends. Friends of this kind are not true friends. What kind of friend are you? Be unwilling to believe a bad report about a person until it is proved. Remain friendly and help even when others do not.

Then God restored the blessing of personal property, giving Job double what he had before.

Figure how much he would have now. This did not necessarily come at once, but gradually as he could rebuild under God's blessing. He again became the richest man in the country. It is likely he also became the most respected again. He had gone through his unusual trial and had been vindicated by God. How valuable the advice of such a man of God should have been!

The most severe blow in the test had been the loss of Job's fine family. Now ten more children were born to Job. If you wonder why the number was not doubled as with the animals, consider this. Children who have died are not lost as animals are. Human souls live on. Job's former children had not ceased to exist. They were not with him on earth, but he would see them in the day of resurrection, an event Job anticipated (19:25-27).

Strange to say, in terms of usual early practice, especially in the Orient, the daughters rather than the sons were magnified as sources of joy for Job. Even their names are given, which was not done for the sons. They are not names girls today would appreciate, but they meant beauty and grace to the father who named them. They were said to have been the most beautiful daughters in the land.

In addition Job gave them an inheritance along with his sons. This was not at all normal. Usually only sons inherited. The daughters' only inheritance came when they married, inheriting sons of another family. In time, God did make a special provision for daughters to inherit if there were no sons (Num. 27:8); but otherwise, daughters did not inherit from their parents.

Finally, God's blessing allowed Job to live 140 years after his suffering experience. It has been suggested that Job may have been seventy years old before his suffering; therefore, his years were doubled also. The age of seventy would fit the fact that his first children were grown and had their own homes. In any case, God added to Job 140 years as a special blessing.

IV. Overall Purpose

The purpose of the Book of Job has been to show the wisdom of trusting God no matter what the circumstances, even when it is impossible to account for them. Job did this, and God greatly rewarded him. Job had suffered at the hand of Satan—not because he was a sinner, but because he was righteous. God permitted it, not as a punishment, but as a test of faith to inspire spiritual growth.

Along the way, you have learned lessons from the speeches of the four friends. The overall lesson is clearly to trust God in all things at all times. God sees and God rewards. His reward may not be in the way or at the time we expect; but He is faithful. When the storms break over you, remember Job's storms. Remember his faithful stand. Remember God's blessing. Therefore, be "stedfast, unmoveable, always abounding in the work of the Lord, forasmuch as ye know that your labour is not in vain in the Lord" (1 Cor. 15:58).

What Is Your Answer?

1. How and when do you think Job found the real reason for his suffering?

2. What is the outstanding lesson you have learned from this study of the Book of Job?

3. Do you intend to continue daily devotional periods?